Download Y[...] Ebook [...]

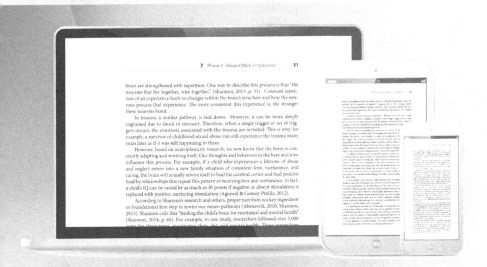

Your print purchase of *Developing Online Learning in the Helping Professions* **includes an ebook download** to the device of your choice—increasing accessibility, portability, and searchability!

Download your ebook today at http://spubonline.com/ollearning and enter the activation code below:

1RL7NSPBS

Angie C. Smith, PhD, LPCS, NCC, has been teaching online within the helping professions for 7 years. She is a teaching associate professor at North Carolina State University, an assistant in the development of the Online Counselor Education Master's Program at North Carolina State University, and coordinator as well as advisor of the College Counseling online program. She is a National Certified Counselor (NCC), Licensed Professional Counselor (LPC), and Licensed Professional Counselor-Supervisor (LPC-S) in North Carolina.

Angie's experience, research, and teaching interests include career counseling and development, online teaching and learning modalities, supervision in counseling, college counseling, student development, group counseling, and technology in the helping professions. Angie has presented at local, state, and national conferences on topics such as group counseling, building community online, and career counseling for adults 50 to 75 years of age. She received a DELTA grant to create an online group counseling course to be offered for the first time at NCSU in this format. She serves on the editorial board for the *Journal of Employment Counseling*, and in 2015 she received the Roy N. Anderson Award for Outstanding Leadership and Service in the Career Development Profession, and she was selected to participate in the Third Annual National Career Development Association Counselor Educator Academy. Her most recent career pursuits include developing and teaching courses for an online master's program at North Carolina State University.

Jeffrey M. Warren, PhD, is an associate professor and chair of the Department of Educational Leadership and Counseling at the University of North Carolina at Pembroke. He received his PhD in counselor education and supervision from North Carolina State University. In 2013, Jeff received the Outstanding Scholar Endowed Award for Research from The Professional Counselor, the flagship journal of the National Board for Certified Counselors (NBCC). He was awarded the Adolph Dial Endowed Award for Scholarship by UNC Pembroke in 2015. The North Carolina Counseling Association recognized him as the 2016 recipient of the Professional Writing and Research Award. In 2017, Jeff received the Counselor Educator of the Year award from the North Carolina School Counselor Association (NCSCA). Jeff's research interests include school consultation, rational emotive behavior therapy, noncognitive factors, teacher beliefs, and school counselor preparation. He has presented at state, national, and international conferences on these topics and has published numerous articles in refereed counseling journals and offered chapters and other contributions to an assortment of counseling-related books. He is a member of the American Counseling Association, the American School Counselor Association, and the Chi Sigma Iota International Honor Society. He serves on the editorial board of The Professional Counselor and the Journal of Rational-Emotive and Cognitive-Behavior Therapy. Jeff is a National Certified Counselor (NCC), a National Certified School Counselor (NCSC), and holds licensure as a professional school counselor and Licensed Professional Counselor Supervisor (LPCS).

Siu-Man R. Ting, PhD, is a professor of counseling, program coordinator of the counselor education program, and the director of Graduate Programs of the Department of Education Leadership, Policy and Human Development, North Carolina State University. Dr. Ting developed the online master's program and the online graduate certificate program at NC State University. He has more than 10 years of experience teaching online.

Dr. Ting studies noncognitive variables and student development, career development, online education, international students, and mental health issues. He is active in scholarly work, consultation, and training nationally and internationally. Dr. Ting has more than 150 publications and presentations. He has developed the Careersbridge.org, which provides free online career assessment and services for people in China. He serves on many editorial boards of professional journals. At present, he is the associate editor of the *Journal of Student Affairs Research and Practice*. In recognition of his research and contributions in noncognitive variables and college student development, he was awarded the Ralph Berdie Research Award of the American Counseling Association in 2005. Also, he is a Fellow of NASPA: Student Affairs Administrators in Higher Education, Scholar of the National Association for College Admission Counseling and the North Carolina College Personnel Association.

Jocelyn D. Taliaferro, PhD, MSW, is an associate professor in the North Carolina State University Department of Social Work. Dr. Taliaferro's current research interests include nonprofit lobbying and teaching using contemporary television. Her work appears in the *Journal of Child and Family Social Work*, the *Journal of Policy Practice*, *Administration in Social Work*, and *Education and Urban Society*. She recently completed a book on teaching social policy using the HBO special *The Wire*.

Prior to her life in academia, Jocelyn spent more than 15 years in the field of social work and nonprofit administration, which included middle and senior management positions. Dr. Taliaferro has been an active member on several nonprofit boards of directors in Washington, DC, Maryland, Delaware, and North Carolina as well as secretary and later chair of the Baltimore City Mayor's Mental Health Advisory Committee. She has been teaching online and hybrid courses since 2006.

Developing Online Learning in the Helping Professions

Online, Blended, and Hybrid Models

Angie C. Smith, PhD, LPCS, NCC
Jeffrey M. Warren, PhD
Siu-Man R. Ting, PhD
Jocelyn D. Taliaferro, PhD, MSW

Editors

SPRINGER PUBLISHING COMPANY

Springer Publishing Company, LLC
11 West 42nd Street
New York, NY 10036
www.springerpub.com

Acquisitions Editor: Sheri W. Sussman
Compositor: S4Carlisle Publishing Services

ISBN: 978-0-8261-8445-0
e-book ISBN: 978-0-8261-8446-7

18 19 20 21 22 / 5 4 3 2 1

The author and the publisher of this Work have made every effort to use sources believed to be reliable to provide information that is accurate and compatible with the standards generally accepted at the time of publication. The author and publisher shall not be liable for any special, consequential, or exemplary damages resulting, in whole or in part, from the readers' use of, or reliance on, the information contained in this book. The publisher has no responsibility for the persistence or accuracy of URLs for external or third-party Internet websites referred to in this publication and does not guarantee that any content on such websites is, or will remain, accurate or appropriate.

Library of Congress Cataloging-in-Publication Data

Names: Smith, Angie C., author.
Title: Developing online learning in the helping professions : online,
    blended, and hybrid models / Angie C. Smith, PhD, LPCS, NCC [and three
    others]
Description: New York : Springer Publishing Company, [2018] | Includes
    bibliographical references and index.
Identifiers: LCCN 2017056191 | ISBN 9780826184450 | ISBN 9780826184467 (ebook)
Subjects: LCSH: Social sciences--Study and teaching (Higher)--Web-based
    instruction. | Social work education--Web-based instruction. | Web-based
    instruction.
Classification: LCC H62.2 .S65 2018 | DDC 361.0071/1--dc23 LC record available at
    https://lccn.loc.gov/2017056191

Contact us to receive discount rates on bulk purchases.
We can also customize our books to meet your needs.
For more information please contact: sales@springerpub.com

Printed in the United States of America.

"Education is one thing that cannot be taken away from you," my wise grandfather shared with me as a child. This book is dedicated to him and his supreme love for learning. Additionally, the book would not have been possible without the love, encouragement, and support of my partner, Jeff Smith, children Hannah, Ella, and Colton, and, of course, all the students who have taught me in many ways throughout the years. Much love and gratitude.

—Angie C. Smith

Hard work and persistence are two of many attributes my parents and grandparents instilled in me. Without their guidance over the years, my efforts to co-author this text would look quite different or may simply not exist. I also must mention the love, support, and encouragement I continually receive from my partner Jenna and two sons Jameson and Jacob. They mean more to me than I can ever express. As such, this book is dedicated to them.

—Jeffrey M. Warren

To my dear wife, Elsa, for her love, tireless support, sacrifice, and creativity.

—Siu-Man R. Ting

This work is dedicated to my grandparents, who admonished me to "Be Somebody," and to my parents, who have encouraged me at every step. A special thank you to my husband, who supports all I do, my coauthors, who were amazing to work with, and my students, who are the entire reason I continue to do this work.

—Jocelyn D. Taliaferro

Contents

Contributors

Amanda Hudson Allen, PhD
Adjunct Teaching Assistant Professor
Department of Educational Leadership, Policy, and Human Development
North Carolina State University
Raleigh, North Carolina

Kimberly Allen, PhD, BCC, CFLE
Associate Professor and Extension Specialist
Department of Agricultural and Human Sciences
North Carolina State University
Raleigh, North Carolina

Tia-Jane'l Bass, DrPH, MPH
Adjunct Assistant Professor
North Carolina Central University
Durham, North Carolina

Cynthia Broderius, MEd
Counselor Education
North Carolina State University
Raleigh, North Carolina

Jodi Brown, MEd
Counselor Education
North Carolina State University
Raleigh, North Carolina

Shanita Brown, PhD
National Certified Counselor and Approved Clinical Supervisor
Visiting Assistant Professor at Wake Forest University
Winston-Salem, North Carolina

Kerri Brown-Parker, MEd
Director, Media and Education Technology Resource Center
North Carolina State University
Raleigh, North Carolina

Nicole Childs, PhD
Teaching Assistant Professor
Graduate Certificate Program in Counselor Education
Department of Educational Leadership, Policy, and Human Development
North Carolina State University
Raleigh, North Carolina

Adria S. Dunbar, PhD
Assistant Professor
Department of Educational Leadership, Policy, and Human Development
North Carolina State University
Raleigh, North Carolina

Elizabeth Grady, MEd, LPCS, NCC, DCC
Graduate Student Teaching Assistant
North Carolina State University
Raleigh, North Carolina

Gabrielle Denise Jones
Graduate Student
North Carolina State University
Raleigh, North Carolina

Shenika Juanita Jones, PhD, MEd
Director of Professional School Counseling Program
Assistant Professor
University of North Carolina at Pembroke
Pembroke, North Carolina

Helen Shulman Lupton-Smith, PhD, MEd, NCC
Clinical Coordinator Counselor Education
Department of Educational Leadership, Policy, and Human Development
North Carolina State University
Raleigh, North Carolina

Jessica L. Oxendine
Graduate Research Assistant
School of Education
University of North Carolina at Pembroke
Pembroke, North Carolina

Jonathan Ryan Ricks, PhD, MA
Assistant Professor
Department of Educational Leadership and Counseling
University of North Carolina at Pembroke
Pembroke, North Carolina

Emily Erin Robinson, EdD, MS
Assistant Director, Office of Faculty Development
North Carolina State University
Raleigh, North Carolina

Jakia Salam, MS
Instructional Designer
Instructional Technology Support and Development
North Carolina State University
Raleigh, North Carolina

Bethany Virginia Smith, MS
Associate Director of Instructional Technology Training
Distance Education and Learning Technology Applications (DELTA)
Adjunct Lecturer, College of Education
North Carolina State University
Raleigh, North Carolina

Rhonda Sutton, PhD, MEd
Adjunct Professor of Counselor Education Program
President of STEPnotes, Inc.
North Carolina State University
Raleigh, North Carolina

Elizabeth A. Vincent, PhD, LPCA, NCC
Assistant Professor
Department of Professional Education
Campbell University
Buies Creek, North Carolina

Courtney B. Walters, MA, LPCS, NCC
Graduate Teaching Assistant
Educational Leadership, Policy, and Human Development—Counselor
  Education
North Carolina State University
Raleigh, North Carolina

Susan H. Ward
Graduate Student
Professional School Counseling
University of North Carolina at Pembroke
Pembroke, North Carolina

Foreword

Online teaching has become more popular than ever before. Although the bulk of college instruction is provided in face-to-face environments, the use of distance or online instruction has steadily increased. Many departments in the helping professions offer at least hybrid or online courses if not entire online programs. The growth and attractiveness of online instruction are manifold. For social work administrators, there are more demands to increase enrollments to meet student demand and interest, even while simultaneously there are fewer resources available to serve these students. Further, more nontraditional students are enrolling in colleges and universities across the country. These students are often older, have caregiver responsibilities, have part- or full-time jobs, and are unable to adhere to the traditional college schedule. At NC State University, most undergraduate classes are offered on Tuesday/Thursday at 10:15 a.m. to 11:30 a.m. That is exactly the time that nontraditional students are unavailable.

Online and hybrid classes address many of these issues. Online classes provide the flexibility for colleges and universities to offer more sections of classes to more students, thereby stretching resources and meeting the needs of students. However, while this may solve some administrative issues, teaching online can be challenging for instructors. Teaching online can be quite labor intensive and frustrating for instructors who may not be fully prepared for the undertaking. Instructors must be able to translate seated class content to the online environment, have strategies to balance the workload, be familiar with technology, and understand how to engage students online. Hence, this book is an essential tool for online instructors.

All too often instructors are assigned an online class with little direction or instruction on how to teach online. This book serves as a companion for instructors regardless of their experience with online teaching: whether they are planning to teach, are first-semester online instructors, or have taught online for many years. This book is designed to help develop a roadmap for the next online class. For instructors who are new to the idea of online instruction, the authors include a chapter that reviews the terminology of the online teaching environment. However, the book also has information about the research on online teaching for those who are more interested in the basis of online instruction rather than the nuts and bolts of implementation.

Information about online teaching is shared in a way that is easily "digestible." An instructor does not have to read the entire book from cover to cover to begin to implement the strategies described. It includes concrete samples and lessons to incorporate, as well as adapt, to fit the online instructor's style, and course offerings are shared by experts in the field. This book is written in a conversational and nonjudgmental tone. The authors do not profess to have all the answers, but instead share their wisdom and guidance freely. Their approach does not preach, lecture, or scold. They even share their own mishaps and bloopers. The tone of the book makes the information easy to consume and relatable.

Another notable feature of the book is the opportunity for reflection and implementation that is offered in each chapter. As a resource for instructors in the helping profession, it provides the chance for readers to assess their own ideas and experiences about teaching while offering additional avenues to explore and enhance their own teaching practices. There are practical, actionable suggestions throughout the book, including methods of keeping students engaged and setting boundaries for the classroom, students, and the instructor. This is one of the most valuable aspects of the book, in that it is truly a guide and not simply a theoretical reflection on online teaching. Instructors can immediately implement the teaching tips and best practices that are offered throughout this book.

Also especially relevant to instructors teaching online in the helping professions is information about ethical standards and best practices. Rightly so, instructors in the helping professions are sensitive to issues of ethics that are associated with online teaching and learning. Some of these issues are highlighted in a practical way using case studies and real-life examples. Just as social work, counselor education, psychology, and other helping professions have codes of ethics, so this book includes a discussion of the ethical considerations for teaching online while providing thoughtful ways of addressing these concerns and relating them to the various professional ethics codes.

Although no book is the single panacea for learning to teach online, this volume is filled with resources, examples, and strategies for teaching online in the helping professions. The book is a guide that will help instructors have a rewarding, stimulating, and satisfying experience with online instruction.

Karen Bullock, PhD, LCSW
Department Head and John A. Hartford Faculty Scholar
Department of Social Work
North Carolina State University
Raleigh, North Carolina

Preface

All four of the authors of this book are professionals in the helping professions. When we started teaching online higher education courses in the helping professions, it felt like we were tossed into the deep end and expected to swim . . . or sink. Assistance, support, instruction, and colleagues with experience in the world of online education hardly existed, so we had to figure it out for ourselves. And we did. But it was challenging, sometimes painful, and always painstaking.

Now we have years of instruction under our belts, and we want to help our colleagues in helping vocations—our fellow gatekeepers for our professions— more efficiently, effectively, and quickly learn the subtle (and not so subtle) ins and outs of online education in our field. A quick Google search will reveal that there are several books in circulation about teaching online, but few focus on the specific challenges and dilemmas that face instructors who teach online courses in psychology, counseling, social work, and other helping vocations where relationships, connection, trust, privacy, and confidentiality are the cornerstones of the field.

In the helping professions, we meet clients where they are in their journeys. Similarly, this book strives to meet you, the reader, right "where you are at" in your quest to learn how to teach in the online environment. Whether your comfort with technology is basic, intermediate, or advanced, you are welcome! Come to this book no matter where you are on your path, because there is always something new to be learned. We even learned a few new ideas from each other in the process of writing the book. We all are continuous learners!

Given the growing prevalence of online learning in the helping professions, we wanted to provide an easy-to-read, research- and experience-based "how to" guide for online instruction. We adopted a multidisciplinary approach, elaborating on the ideas, practices, teaching and learning strategies, new technologies, best practices, and ethical issues for administrators and instructors as well as students, as student-centered education is a vital component of helping professional education.

We invite you to participate and reflect on each topic, and we offer vignettes, reflective questions, checklists, examples, bullet points, timelines, tips, and takeaways to support your growth and development as an instructor and the development of your online courses and programs.

Chapters 1 and 2 set the foundation for your new endeavor and familiarize new online instructors with the fundamental technology and practical applications of delivering content online within the helping fields. This includes a review of basic education platforms and a glossary of key terms and definitions. These are the words, jargon, and terminology that you will need to know as you begin to learn about online education.

In Chapter 3, we address the typical fears and anxieties associated with teaching online in the helping vocations, including unfamiliarity with technology, and we offer approaches that can smooth ruffled emotions so that you can stress less and confidently deliver your online course.

In Chapter 4, the authors focus on the student experience and perspectives of online courses based on a brief guided questionnaire of open-ended questions offered to our learners. What is the most important factor for online student success and satisfaction? Find out!

What does current social science research and helping professions literature have to say about the efficacy of online education and delivery methods? In Chapter 5, the authors survey the research into online education and address the quality concerns associated with online classes and programs, demonstrating their effectiveness.

We move from theory to the super practical in Chapter 6, where we present a roadmap of practical steps for course design and building, tech-tool use, communication techniques, and many more considerations for a successful semester. We guide the new online instructor (and administrator) through a detailed list of steps to take for building online courses and a timeline for successful course design, planning, development, and implementation. What do you need to *know* and what do you need to *do* to get your course up and running in one month or less? We show you how.

In Chapter 7, the authors address practical tips to learners themselves, and provide useful samples for instructors to use in preparing them to become online learners; we also include tips that were developed by graduate students in online education programs. These samples are effective tools for novice students and others who are new to the online learning environment.

In Chapter 8, we provide tips and best practices from experts in the helping field; the professional literature offers a wide range of research studies that can inform online programs (administrators, instructors, and staff) about best practices. We know that developing a new online course or program can be overwhelming for new online instructors, requiring instructors to learn to use related technologies, design a curriculum, develop learning modules of the right size, plan for learning activities, and design tests and examinations.

In Chapter 9, we join with additional contributors who also teach online courses within the helping professions to share samples, templates, ethical considerations, standards of practice, and examples from both Blackboard Collaborate (synchronous) meetings and asynchronous platforms. These examples are aligned with the core standards within the helping professions. This chapter provides the reader with "ready-made" activities, examples, and resources that can be used, adapted, and repurposed when developing and delivering a course.

In Chapter 10, entitled "What NOT to Do," we walk you through some common pitfalls—along with the pits we fell in—and present recommendations on what not to do based on our experiences and those of other online instructors in the helping professions.

Ethics and academic integrity are the central subjects of Chapter 11. We focus on the ethical considerations in online teaching alongside the distinctiveness and importance of integrity in our field, recognizing that privacy, confidentiality, and trust are the foundation of our work. The chapter highlights ethical standards, clinical work, variations on teaching online, student ethics, and practical case studies and vignettes.

Education- and communication-centered technology are changing rapidly, so it is vital for online instructors to continue to update their knowledge and skills in those technologies. In Chapter 12, we look at the evolving technological environment around online learning. Colleagues at the Distance Education and Learning Technology Applications (DELTA) department at North Carolina State University, who are experts in instructional design and technology within the college setting, share concrete examples and describe the discussions they engage in when working with both new and seasoned instructors who are delivering content online.

The authors then look ahead at trends and opportunities in online teaching and learning in Chapter 13, presenting several practical tools, software, apps, and platforms for the reader to consider using to enhance the online class experience.

Finally, in Chapter 14, the authors provide encouragement to readers who are beginning the process of course design and delivery. In this final chapter, we include a To Do list for preparing your online course and semester.

Acknowledgments

Thank you to all who contributed to the creation of the book. A publication is not created in a vacuum and it takes the hard work and dedication of so many individuals to collectively make it happen. We are eternally grateful for the support of colleagues, our institutions, friends, and family. We would like to thank the following colleagues and departments for their continuous support and encouragement: MaryAnn Danowitz, Ellen Vasu, Penny Pasque, Stacy Gant, and Lacey Bloom, as well as the Distance Education and Learning Technology Applications (DELTA), Educational Leadership, Policy, and Human Development (ELPHD) at North Carolina State University and Alfred Bryant, Angela McDonald, and the Department of Educational Leadership and Counseling at the University of North Carolina at Pembroke. Last, but certainly not least, we would like to thank our students for sharing their time, energy, and feedback with all of us so that we can continue to learn and grow as online instructors and helping professionals. We are grateful for all the unique contributions you bring to the profession and classroom!

CHAPTER 1

Introduction to Online Teaching in the Helping Professions: Where Do You Fit In?

OVERARCHING QUESTIONS

1. What are your goals for online teaching?
2. What are you looking for in this book that will support your online teaching goals?
3. Have you taught an online class or taken an online class before?
4. Where are your gaps in knowledge?
5. What resources do you need to effectively teach your course?
6. Who do you know in the field who teaches online courses?
7. What resources are available in and around your institution that can support your online teaching practice?

So, you want to teach an online course or in an online program . . .

Okay, maybe you are reluctant, but you have been charged with developing an online program or teaching a course online. Now you are looking for help and direction on how and where to start this journey. It's okay if you are feeling a little overwhelmed or stumped on where to start—we have been there and we are here to help.

Our hope for you, as you read this book, is that you will examine who you are as a person and instructor. As you do so, begin to consider your identity as an online instructor within the helping professions. What do you already bring to the course? How will you share your gifts, knowledge, and expertise in the online space?

We, the authors, have been teaching online courses for a collective 23 years. Through the years and through all the courses we've taught, we have made tons of errors and mistakes, discovered what works and what doesn't, grappled with personal challenges, took blind leaps of faith into innovative technology, developed new ways of being and relating online, and learned to embrace online modes of instruction and modeling to our students. From our experiences, we have "gathered our thoughts" for online teaching success with good outcomes for our students.

Let us take you by the hand and walk this journey with you. We will share our experiences and help you think through course design, requisite technology, and helpful resources to smooth your transition. We also offer tips, tricks, activities, exercises, and personal points of reflection to get you started.

Buckle up and enjoy the ride as we navigate teaching and learning online.

■ Why Online Education?

Online learning is a hot topic. It is one of the fastest growing trends in the educational use of technology:

- The National Center for Education Statistics reported that 12,153,000 online students are enrolled in in postsecondary, credit-granting courses (Parsad, Lewis, & Tice, 2008).

- Technology-based distance learning in K–12 public schools grew by about 65% between 2002 and 2005, and in 2007 more than 1 million K–12 students took online courses (Picciano & Seaman, 2007).

- In the fall of 2010, more than 6.1 million students were taking at least one online course (Bart, 2011).

- 31% of all higher education students now take at least one course online (Allen & Seaman, 2011).

Currently, online education programs are typically asynchronous; the technology used for these courses includes emails, discussion forums, article reviews, and narrated slides or film clips (Brown, 2002, p. 9; Vogel & Klassen, 2001, pp. 104–114; Yang & Cornelious, 2004). However, recent improvement in synchronous teaching technology means that more interactive discussions, assignments, and exercises can be built into the course design. For example, some courses use web conferencing or virtual meetings via Blackboard Collaborate, Adobe Connect, and other synchronous platforms (Rockinson-Szapkiw & Walker, 2009, pp. 175–193; Smith et al., 2015, pp. 47–57; Ting, 2016).

The recent explosion of online classes and programs in higher education in the United States is attributed to shortages in classroom space and facilities due to rapid growth in the student population. Developing new online programs is far more cost-effective than constructing new buildings. Also, the growing numbers of nontraditional students, including working adults, often find it challenging to commute to campus to attend face-to-face classes. Some students live in a remote area or far from campus, or they may have family, work, or other commitments that prevent them from taking on-campus classes. For these students, online programs enable them to take classes wherever they are and usually without time limitations—although virtual class meetings for students in faraway time zones may make attendance a challenge.

Online education and technology make new demands on instructors, of course, but they also put unique demands on students. Students enrolled in online classes can study at their own pace by following a weekly study schedule or following topical learning modules, and they usually only need a desktop or laptop computer with Internet access to take the course.

Online education is a better match for some personalities and learning types than for others. It works especially well for students who are self-disciplined, independent learners who are flexible, open to using technology, willing to take initiative, and able to work in groups (Schwitzer, Ancis, & Brown, 2001[1]).

■ Online Education in the Helping Professions

The growing popularity of online learning extends to the helping professions. In the United States, there are 34 online master's programs in counselor education are listed on the Council for Accreditation of Counseling and Related Educational Programs (CACREP) website. In social work education, there are at least 15 baccalaureate-level programs and 63 master's programs that are fully or mostly online, according to the Council on Social Work Education.

The benefits of moving courses into the virtual world in the helping professions are similar to those in other programs: flexibility of scheduling, ability to reach students in distant locations, fewer demands on physical classroom space on campus, and self-paced student learning that focuses on areas that the student finds especially interesting (El Mansour & Mupinga, 2007, pp. 242–248). However, there is interesting research suggesting that online forums may be *especially* helpful in our field. One study offered that today's technological natives are really comfortable in digital-land, and that students are willing to disclose more when they are not in a physical classroom of peers (Trepal, Haberstroh, Duffey, & Evans, 2007, pp. 226–279). The anonymity of virtual meetings has the social function of a mask at a carnival, offering "certain kinds of relief from [those] massive pressures that societies place on individuals" (Oravec, 1996, p. 153).

Our hope is that this book will be a companion manual for you to read and reread as you learn and experiment with your online courses and programs. The nature of the book invites you into the process by reflecting on your own experiences as an individual, instructor, and helping professional. You will notice throughout the book that we have included guided questions and reflective prompts to help you to consider how you might use the information the authors share with you.

Let's get started . . .

---

[1] This matches well with findings from another similar study:

Clingerman, T. L., & Bernard, J. M. (2004). An investigation of e-mail as a supplemental modality for clinical supervision. *Counselor Education and Supervision, 43*, 82–95. doi:10.1002/j.1556-6978.2004.tb01862.x

■ Guided Prompts

1. Why did you select this book to read?

    _____

    _____

2. What do you hope to learn by reading the content of the book?

    _____

    _____

3. Where do you feel like you are beginning as an online instructor?

    _____

    _____

4. As a helping professional, what are you most curious about learning in the online environment?

    _____

    _____

5. What do you already know about teaching in the online, hybrid, and/ or blended models?

    _____

    _____

HELPFUL TIP: You might have noticed that online learning is called by a variety of names. Terms such as *online learning, e-learning, distance learning, e-courses, distance education*, and *online instruction* all refer to the process of teaching via an online teaching platform.

"Will it be easy? Nope. Worth it? Absolutely."—Unknown.

Resources

Anderson, K., & May, F. A. (2010). Does the method of instruction matter? An experimental examination of information literacy instruction in the online, blended, and face-to-face classrooms. *The Journal of Academic Librarianship, 36*(6), 495–500. doi:10.1016/j.acalib.2010.08.005

Artino, A. R. (2010). Online or face-to-face learning? Exploring the personal factors that predict students' choice of instructional format. *The Internet and Higher Education, 13*(4), 272–276. doi:10.1016/j.iheduc.2010.07.005

Collins, S., & Jerry, P. (2005). The Campus Alberta Applied Psychology Counselling Initiative: Web-based delivery of a graduate professional training program. *Journal of Technology in Human Services, 23*(1&2), 99–119. doi:10.1300/J017v23n01_07

References

Allen, I. E., & Seaman, J. (2011). *Going the distance: Online education in the United States*. Newburyport, MA: Sloan Consortium. Retrieved from http://www.babson.edu/Academics/centers/blank-center/global-research/Documents/going-the-distance.pdf

Bart, M. (2011, December 2). More than six million students learning online, study finds. *Faculty Focus*. Retrieved from https://www.facultyfocus.com/articles/edtech-news-and-trends/more-than-6-million-students-learning-online-study-finds

Brown, D. G. (2002). The role you play in online discussion. *Syllabus, 16*(5), 9. Retrieved from: https://campustechnology.com/Articles/2002/11/The-Role-you-Play-in-Online-Discussions.aspx

Clingerman, T. L., & Bernard, J. M. (2004). An investigation of the use of e-mail as a supplemental modality for clinical supervision. *Counselor Education and Supervision, 44*, 82–95. doi:10.1002/j.1556-6978.2004.tb01862.x

El Mansour, B., & Mupinga, D. M. (2007). Students' positive and negative experiences in hybrid and online classes. *College Student Journal, 41*(1), 242–248. Retrieved from ERIC database. Eric Document EJ765422.

Oravec, J. A. (1996). *Virtual individuals, virtual groups: Human dimensions of groupware and computer networking*. Cambridge, UK: Cambridge University Press.

Parsad, B., Lewis, L., & Tice, P. (2008). *Distance education at degree-granting postsecondary institutions: 2006-07*. Washington, DC: National Center for Education Statistics. Retrieved from https://nces.ed.gov/pubs2009/2009044.pdf

Picciano, A. G., & Seaman, J. (2007). *K–12 online learning: A survey of U.S. school district administrators*. Boston, MA: Sloan Consortium. Retrieved from http://www.sloan-c.org/publications/survey/K-12_06

Rockinson-Szapkiw, A. J., & Walker, V. L. (2009). Web 2.0 technologies: Facilitating interaction in an online human services counseling skills course. *Journal of Technology in Human Services, 27*(3), 175–193. doi:10.1080/15228830903093031

Schwitzer, A. M., Ancis, J. R., & Brown, N. (2001). *Promoting student learning and student development at a distance: Student affairs concepts and practices for televised instruction and other forms of distance education*. Lanham, MD: American College Personnel Association.

Smith, R. L., Flamez, B., Vela, J. C., Schomaker, S. A., Fernandez, M. A., & Armstrong, S. N. (2015). An exploratory investigation of levels of learning and learning efficiency between online and face-to-face instruction. *Counseling Outcome Research and Evaluation, 6*(1), 47–57. doi:10.1177/2150137815572148

Ting, S. R. (2016, September). *Evaluation of an online counseling program*. Paper presented at the Eleventh International Conference on Teaching, Education, and Learning, London, UK.

Trepal, H., Haberstroh, S., Duffey, T., & Evans, M. (2007). Considerations and strategies for teaching online counseling skills: Establishing relationships in cyberspace. *Counselor Education and Supervision, 46*(4), 266–279. doi:10.1002/j.1556-6978.2007.tb00031.x

Vogel, D., & Klassen, J. (2001). Technology-supported learning: Status, issues and trends. *Journal of Computer Assisted Learning, 17*(1), 104–114. doi:10.1111/j.1365-2729.2001.00163.x

Yang, Y., & Cornelious, L. F. (2004, October). *Ensuring quality in online education instructions: What instructors should know?* Paper presented at the annual meeting of the Association for Educational Communications and Technology, Chicago, IL. Retrieved from ERIC database. ERIC Document ED484990.

CHAPTER 2

Learning the Online Teaching Language: Key Terms and Definitions

Technology evolves at a rapid pace. Higher education has adapted to these technological advances and employed them to enhance course offerings and provide access for students seeking postsecondary certificates, programs, and degrees. This may explain why distance education course offerings and online learning are more prevalent than ever.

Online learning entails the application of the Internet during provision of instruction in a specific field or preparation program. According to the U.S. Department of Education, during the 2003 to 2004 academic year 15.6% of undergraduate students were enrolled in an online course and 4.9% were enrolled in a degree program delivered completely via distance education. However, in the fall of 2013, 15.6% of students were enrolled in an online course, while 13.1% took all online courses (U.S. Department of Education, 2016). The trend of online learning in higher education will likely continue as new and innovative practices in distance education emerge.

The evolution of distance education in postsecondary settings has led to fundamental shifts in the ways that courses are delivered, instructors interact with students, and students are evaluated. Some students excitedly enroll in distance education courses and are poised with the knowledge, attitudes, and skills to be quite successful in navigating the nuances of online learning. Alternately, other students are met with hesitation and have reservations about learning in online formats. A lack of technological competence, and often a steep learning curve, can result in anxiety and frustration for learners. These experiences and feelings related to distance education may also be relevant for instructors.

REFLECTIVE CHECKLIST

The following is a brief questionnaire designed to help you gauge your familiarity with technology. Simply, the more questions you can confidently answer with a "YES," the more likely it is that you are equipped with the knowledge, attitudes, and skills to be successful as an online instructor.

☐   1. Technology has always been a part of my life.

☐   2. I frequently use social media to engage with family, friends, and others.

☐   3. I participate in webinars and teleconferences.

☐   4. I have my own website or web space.

☐   5. I can easily navigate and search a topic on the Internet.

☐   6. I have a smartphone and use it for more than phone calls.

☐   7. I have heard of Second Life or another virtual world.

☐   8. I have checked in at the airport electronically and used a kiosk to print my tickets.

☐   9. I frequently purchase items online (e.g., groceries, clothing).

☐ 10. I cannot imagine life without technology.

The most fundamental tool in online education is called a learning management system (LMS) or course management system (CMS). Blackboard and Moodle are the two LMSs most frequently used by programs that prepare students for the helping professions. We introduce you to how LMSs are used in online education and briefly describe additional ancillary online tools and applications. The chapter concludes with a glossary of terms and definitions online instructors must become familiar with for success and a list of supplemental resources to help introduce you to the basics of online instruction.

■ Delivery Modes of Online Instruction

In a broad sense, online instruction in higher education is delivered either synchronously or asynchronously. Classes that are offered online in a synchronous format meet virtually on a specific day and at a specific time. For example, a synchronous course on multicultural issues and social justice may meet virtually each Monday of the semester from 6:00 p.m. to 8:30 p.m. An asynchronous class will never meet together "live," at the same time, as a group.

All Asynchronous

In the asynchronous course, the student is self-paced and engages with the content and material in the LMS based on the due dates for assignments, papers, quizzes, and so forth. In these classes, the level of support from instructors varies. One significant difference between all-synchronous and all-asynchronous courses is the instructor's availability; synchronous courses offer a live format to respond and answer questions. In asynchronous courses, most interaction occurs via email or maybe phone, unless the instructor offers to meet via Skype or other "live" session for meetings.

Instructors who employ an asynchronous format do not meet with students at a designated time each week. Instead, students enrolled in an asynchronous course can complete assignments online throughout the week based on their personal schedules. These online courses typically are driven by deadlines and due dates. For example, the instructor may outline on the course syllabus that the Week 5 Learning Module, which includes select readings, three discussion threads, and a quiz, must be completed by noon on Friday. Some instructors may elect to offer modified formats such as a combination of synchronous and asynchronous class meetings throughout the semester.

WORD TO THE WISE: If a course is offered asynchronously but requires one or more virtual or face-to-face meetings too, these meeting dates and their format should be clearly outlined on the course syllabus and scheduled well in advance.

One research has noted several distinctions between asynchronous and face-to-face instruction (including synchronous learning); these differences are relevant almost two decades later (Tiene, 2000, pp. 369–382). For example, access to other students and the course instructor may be limited or students may simply perceive that access is limited. Asynchronous courses often create delayed responses and "drawn-out" dialog given the variability in students' schedules and their flexibility in completing assignments. As a result, some students who expect more immediate responses may experience frustration or become disconnected from the evolving dialog in the discussion threads.

Other factors such as expression and visual cues are influenced by course format and affect the student's instructional experience. A more recent study also described the differences between modes or formats of online instruction (Wang & Woo, 2007, pp. 272–286). The authors noted that factors such as efficiency, rate of response, quality of communication, and overall atmosphere are influenced by course format. It is important for instructors to consider these variables as course formats are considered. Furthermore, instructors must acknowledge the role facilitation has on student interactions and experiences. It is imperative that online instructors create optimal learning environments for all students.

Hybrid

Hybrid courses involve both online and face-to-face meetings, and there are many variations in the ways courses may be offered. The frequency of the on-campus meeting may vary depending on the institution, instructor, or requirements for your program. A few examples include:

- Courses offered on-campus once a week and content is offered simultaneously in the LMS for students to complete at their own pace.

- An on-campus meeting may be required once a month for a one- or two-day weekend session in addition to the material covered asynchronously online.
- Once a semester, instructors require a meeting similar to a workshop session in addition to the semester-long content covered in the asynchronous environment (i.e., Moodle).

In hybrid classes, the level of engagement of the instructor may be more visible and active, as students will attend on-campus and live sessions in person. After-class meetings or impromptu meetings before or after class may be a possibility, too.

Combination of Asynchronous and Synchronous Learning

A combination approach to course design provides multiple opportunities for students to engage with the instructor and content. Students are offered course material, lectures, and assignments in the asynchronous platform and join "live" sessions on the synchronous platform. Students can meet in virtual sessions with the instructor and fellow students to practice skills, cover content, ask questions, and learn from one another. For example, students may be required to read assignments in the LMS, then come to a virtual class session to discuss what they learned and then apply the content to "real-life" scenarios. The instructor can engage with students in the virtual online environment through discussions, breakout sessions for group work, lectures, office hours, and other activities.

Flipped Classrooms

In this classroom model, the typical elements of a course are reversed. Lectures are viewed at home or on the student's own time before the class, and class time is reserved for participatory projects, skills practice, role play, and small/large group discussions.

▪ Learning Management Systems

There are many platforms and programs available for instructors to use when delivering online instruction. Instructors who use a variety of teaching methods, tools, and programs will likely engage students more easily. There are many LMS suites available that offer a host of options for developing and delivering online courses. Several of these LMSs are described here.

Essentially all universities and programs of higher education that offer distance education have invested in an LMS. An LMS is a powerful software application that provides instructors and students with the interface for optimal online learning.
Most LMSs:

- Offer enhanced management features
- Deliver a platform for creating and disseminating learning content quickly

- Provide resources to enhance efficiency and sufficiency
- Are universally accessible and compatible

Options for LMSs have expanded with the evolution of distance education. The most common LMSs in helping profession and education training programs are Blackboard and Moodle. Other emerging LMS software applications include Braincert.com and JoomlaLMS. The LMS used by the instructor is mostly likely dictated by the institution's supported platform.

Blackboard

Blackboard is an online learning suite that offers an assortment of products and services. Most of these features are used asynchronously. The built-in discussion boards, wikipages, group space, assignment submission portals, email messaging systems, and assessment tools are frequently used by instructors to facilitate learning.

Course content is delivered in learning modules. *Learning modules* are organized packages of content that may include readings, assignments, and discussion threads, based on a certain topic explored within a course. These modules are commonly developed by instructors and use various features and tools that facilitate learning. Videos and hyperlinks to external sources are often embedded in the learning modules as well.

Blackboard also offers a web-conferencing application called "Collaborate." Blackboard Collaborate synchronously connects instructors and students for real-time, online instruction. Features of this web-conferencing app include bidirectional audio and video functionality, chatting, a recording option, screen sharing, and the ability to display PowerPoint presentations and other documents. Instructors can also create virtual breakout rooms for students to work together in small groups. The instructor has the ability to display the small groups' white boards for large-group discussion. Instructors can use Collaborate to hold interactive class discussions or to meet individually with students.

Moodle

Moodle is open-source software used by many universities to deliver online courses and programs. Moodle is free, but the platform does require setup and formatting that necessitate support beyond the expertise of the instructor. Course instructors do have access and privileges with Moodle to develop, design, and customize courses as needed to optimize learning outcomes.

The features of Moodle include a lesson planner, discussion forums, wikis, file sharing, automatic content management, and collaboration activities. Instructors can use Moodle to track attendance, monitor the roster, assess student knowledge, and disseminate grades. Messaging and chat features are also available, which allows additional opportunities for communication and interaction with and between students.

Other LMSs include:

- Eliademy: www.eliademy.com
- Adobe Captivate Prime: www.adobe.com
- Docebo: www.docebo.com
- Schoology: www.schoology.com
- Absorb: www.absorblms.com
- Edmodo: www.edmodo.com
- Canvas: www.canvaslms.com
- D2L: www.d2l.com

■ Online Tools for Learning

There are many LMSs available in the marketplace. Each has appeal as well as limitations. However, unless serving as a member of a technology or distance education-focused committee, instructors typically have little input in the decision to adopt a university-wide LMS. As a result, the adopted LMS may fail to meet the needs or preferences of all instructors. To fill such gaps, instructors may elect to incorporate or embed additional technologies or applications to meet student-learning outcomes.

There are many stand-alone applications that have educational value that are readily available to instructors. We have reviewed several of these tools and applications in Chapter 13.

■ Online Instruction: Is It Good for the Instructor?

What is the opportunity cost to faculty for teaching online?

Faculty with multiple obligations may seek online teaching opportunities for the same reasons as students, and while it may be a wonderful opportunity, it does come with costs.

The value of teaching online varies by the institution. At teaching institutions, teaching an online course may be of high value, as it is an opportunity for innovative instruction and connection with students. However, at research-intensive institutions, innovative teaching is of relatively low value. Research institutions value the scholarly output of articles, book chapters, and books, and teaching online often requires more time than teaching a seated class, which takes time away from scholarship and research productivity.

Instructors in tenure track positions have to give significant consideration to the benefits and rewards of devoting the amount of time it takes to develop and deliver an online course if a seated class would do. It is important to think intentionally about its impact on tenure and promotion. Consider having a conversation with your department head and the department's voting faculty that will ultimately vote or decide on granting tenure.

Is the cost of teaching a flexible, interesting, innovative course too high? Administrators should talk very candidly with online teaching faculty to ensure they have considered the long-term career ramifications of this choice.

▪ Glossary of Useful Terms and Concepts

There are numerous terms used in the delivery of online learning. The list provided here is not exhaustive. However, the list does provide the reader with a basic overview of important concepts all online instructors should know and understand. Each term is defined and includes a statement about its relevance to online learning.

Bandwidth. *Bandwidth* is a term used to describe the amount of data an Internet connection can support over a certain period of time. It is usually reported in megabytes per second (Mbps). An Internet connection with a high bandwidth can download and upload data faster than one with a low bandwidth. Given the size of documents, videos, and synchronous tools used in online instruction, instructors must consider their bandwidth as well as their students' bandwidth connection. Students with a low bandwidth connection may have difficulty participating in synchronous mode and experience delays when downloading documents or videos.

Blended learning. *Blended learning* is a broad term that can include a mixture of modes of instruction. This term includes hybrid courses but also can encompass the mixing of synchronous and asynchronous modes of online learning. A course offered in the classroom on three Saturdays out of the semester with weekly asynchronous learning and monthly synchronous sessions is representative of blended learning.

Blogs. Blogs are often small websites developed by individuals. These websites often include personal accounts, tips, and ideas covering a variety of topics. Blogs are often developed using basic programming strategies and are maintained/hosted for free in many cases. Blogs can be used in numerous ways to engage students and foster interactive discussions.

Chat. Chatting is a common feature across social media, web conferencing, and LMS use. Chatting via pop-up windows or rooms allows multiple users to hold brief and often informal discussion in real time. The discussion thread is easy to access and follow. Instructors can use chat or messaging features during synchronous instruction for lectures, for troubleshooting technology issues, or for encouraging students to engage in interactive discussions.

Cloud. Cloud is a storage space that allows users to upload files for easy access. Files housed in the cloud are accessible to any computer from which the user signs into the storage space. Clouds are especially useful when files are too large for sharing via email. In this case, the file can be uploaded to the cloud and shared with the appropriate party. Dropbox and Google Drive are two commonly used cloud storage services. Instructors can use cloud services to store course documents, develop libraries, and share selected files or folders with students. Students can also use a cloud service to upload assignments, such as video demonstrations, to share with a course instructor.

Discussion boards. Discussion boards are online tools for posting messages or responding to a message or request. This exchange of information and ideas occurs asynchronously in most cases. Instructors may post questions on a discussion board for students to answer after reading a chapter or completing a learning module.

Download versus upload. Downloading occurs when a file is transferred from a website or server to a local computer. Uploading occurs when a file on a local computer is transferred to a website or server. An online instructor may upload the course syllabus to an LMS, so that students can download it to their computers for offline access.

Emoticons. *Emoticons* or *emojis* are images or pictures that exemplify emotions, moods, and common everyday activities. Depending on the technology, some users use letters and numbers to create emoticons, whereas others can simply select from a variety of images. Instructors can use emoticons in numerous ways, including quick, positive feedback such as "Nice job!:+)"

Gamification. Gamification is an emerging trend in education. This term describes the implementation of game-based theory, strategies, and techniques in nongame environments such as online instruction. An example of gamification is the use of simple rewards or tokens embedded in a learning module to increase participation and engagement.

Host/Server. These terms are defined in very similar ways. Without getting too technical, a *server* is a piece of software that provides users with information or resources upon request. Most universities maintain servers that faculty access to retrieve information. These servers host websites, email clients, and databases that allow information to be neatly organized and easily accessed. Instructors simply need to understand these concepts, as universities often upgrade or patch servers routinely, which can intermittently interrupt instruction.

Hybrid course. This is a mode of instructional delivery that includes a combination of online learning and classroom meetings. The online portion of a hybrid course is either synchronous or asynchronous and is typically used to supplement the class portion.

Hyperlink. Hyperlinks are addresses or data references embedded in a word, phrase, or image that redirect users to new information upon clicking. When developing a learning module, instructors can create hyperlinks to send students to a site for additional information. For example, in a lesson on attention deficit hyperactivity disorder (ADHD), students who click on the hyperlinked phrase "Learn more about ADHD" are redirected to www.chadd.org.

Instant messaging. See Chat.

Learning modules. Learning modules are often housed in LMSs. Modules are developed to provide students with structure and direction for asynchronously completing a lesson or unit on a designated topic. They allow students to sequentially complete tasks that often lead to a culminating assignment, such as discussion posts or a quiz. For example, online instructors can develop learning models that include a topic overview, module goals and objectives, videos, PowerPoint slides, interactive discussion threads, and a mini quiz.

Link rot. Websites and their addresses are ever-changing. Link rot occurs when a link or particular web address no longer accesses information it once did. At the beginning of each semester, instructors must remain diligent in ensuring that the links provided in syllabi and learning modules direct students to the intended information. This is particularly important when instructors recycle resources from previous semesters.

Listservs. Listservs allow users to disperse information quickly and efficiently to an organized group. Subscribers typically have the option to receive messages immediately or in a digest format. Many university departments maintain separate listservs for faculty and students. Faculty often use this mode of communication to distribute important dates or events to students enrolled in a particular program.

Lurking. *Lurking*, a social media term, occurs when someone enters a discussion board or chat room and reads the posts or comments without responding. Instructors can lurk on discussion boards to ensure that students are responding thoroughly and in appropriate ways to the discussion prompts.

MOOC: An acronym for massive open online courses; MOOCs are online platforms that typically offer free self-paced instruction.

Netiquette. Similar to etiquette, this term describes the respectful manner in which interactions should occur between students and between the student and the instructor. It is important for instructors to demonstrate netiquette and review netiquette expectations at the beginning of the online course.

Radio buttons. Also called options buttons, these allow the user to choose one option out of a selection of options. Most LMSs offer radio buttons that can be used by students and instructors to enhance participation in the online environment.

Remote. *Remote* describes distance and the way that users access information. In online instruction, information and data are exchanged remotely over a network or a server.

Router versus modem. A modem establishes a connection with a designated Internet service provider (ISP). Computers and laptops can be connected directly to the modem for wired access using an ethernet cable. A router is useful for establishing wireless Internet connections with various forms of technology (e.g., laptops, tablets, and smartphones). Wired access typically offers a stronger, and in most cases more secure, connection. It is important that instructors understand how to troubleshoot these pieces of hardware when they are unable to secure an Internet connection. If the instructor is unable to remedy a problematic Internet connection, having a plan B as a backup is a good idea.

Search engine. Search engines are commonplace, and oftentimes considered a starting point when seeking information on a certain topic. Google, Bing, and Yahoo are popular search engines that scan the Internet, index information, and then retrieve it when prompted by keywords.

Social media. This term is used to describe any website or application that allows users to interact or communicate with society at large. Popular social media include Facebook, Instagram, Twitter, and Pinterest. Online instructors can incorporate these media tools into weekly lessons or assignments. For example, students can create Twitter accounts and post statistics and information about mental health to practice advocacy.

Virtual world. Virtual worlds are online, simulated communities where users interact with each other using avatars (icons or figures). These 3D worlds allow users, through their avatars, to connect with others in dance clubs, at university campuses, in libraries, or at a conference or symposium. Instructors should consider how virtual worlds can be used to enhance distance education.

Virus. A *virus* is a small program or sequence of code that has the potential to destroy data and debilitate technology including computers, laptops, and smartphones connected to the Internet. Viruses often replicate and can spread easily via email, downloads, and sharing of flash drives. It is important for instructors to maintain security features on their devices that minimize the potential for acquiring a virus.

VoIP. This acronym stands for "voice over Internet Protocol." VoIP describes the ability of users to speak to others via the Internet rather than by traditional telephone. Many applications and websites offer VoIP features today. This method of communication allows instructors and students the option to engage in synchronous, voiced discussions as opposed to chatting by text.

Webcasting. Many live events are broadcast over the Internet as a webcast. Individuals can remotely view the event when provided with a link. Webcasts are often recorded and housed on relevant websites for later viewing. Instructors can include live or recorded webcasts of events relevant to instruction.

Web page versus website. Web addresses direct individuals to a specific location on the Internet. For example, www.counseling.org leads to the "home" web page for the website of the American Counseling Association. A website can contain many web pages that are often accessible from the home page of the site. It is important for instructors to use the correct terminology when directing students to web pages or sites.

Wikis. There are myriad wikis available on the Internet today. Similar to a "living encyclopedia," these sites allow users from around the world to alter, revise, or create content about a specific topic. The information contained in these websites continues to grow and evolve. Much of the information available on these sites is reviewed and monitored for accuracy. However, readers are encouraged to verify the information using a third party (i.e., direct source). Some LMSs offer a wiki that instructors can use to facilitate group projects or offer editable information about a topic.

REFLECTIVE QUESTIONS

1. What technology are you currently using?
2. Where can you obtain training to enhance your instructional skills?
3. How do you intend to incorporate technology into your curriculum, teaching, and course(s) this semester, this year, and in the future?

HELPFUL TIP: New technology is developed and released on a daily basis. Current programs and applications are often updated or fixes are issued to address "bugs." Stay up-to-date on the latest technology trends by visiting sites such as www.campustechnology.com. It is also helpful to adjust program and application settings to allow automatic updates.

"Without language, one cannot talk to people and understand them; one cannot share their hopes and aspirations, grasp their history, appreciate their poetry, or savour their songs."—Nelson Mandela

Resources

Ellis, R. K. (2009). *Field guide to learning management systems.* American Society for Training & Development (ASTD) Learning Circuits. Retrieved from https://www.astd.org/~/media/Files/Publications/LMS_fieldguide_20091

References

Tiene, D. (2000). Online discussions: A survey of advantages and disadvantages compared to face-to-face discussions. *Journal of Educational Multimedia and Hypermedia, 9*(4), 369–382. Retrieved from http://www.learntechlib.org/p/9551

U.S. Department of Education. (2016). *Digest of education statistics, 2014* (NCES 2016-006). National Center for Education Statistics. Retrieved from https://nces.ed.gov/pubs2016/2016006.pdf

Wang, Q., & Woo, H. L. (2007). Comparing asynchronous online discussions and face-to-face discussions in a classroom setting. *British Journal of Educational Technology, 38*(2), 272–286. doi:10.1111/j.1467-8535.2006.00621.x

CHAPTER 3

Helping the Helper: Allaying Fears of the Online Environment

OVERARCHING QUESTIONS

1. What strengths do I possess that translate to the online learning environment?
2. What deficits do I possess that may hinder my attempts to deliver online instruction?
3. How do I determine success in the online learning environment?
4. How do I respond to challenges or adversities in life and in the classroom?

Just the thought of providing online instruction can feel stressful and anxiety-ridden. Developing and delivering online courses can feel especially overwhelming when little or no guidance or support is provided.

Instructors bring their own strengths as well as their deficits to the online learning environment, where some of these strengths and deficits are magnified. Course content and how it is delivered online can also present unique challenges, especially for instructors with limited knowledge of or experience with the medium. Even those experienced in delivering online instruction can face unexpected challenges.

Online teaching requires planning, focus, diligence, thoughtfulness, and attention to detail to the curriculum and instruction. This chapter explores the variables that can ultimately determine the success or failure of the online instructor. We offer strategies that can help instructors manage thoughts and emotions and minimize stress.

VIGNETTES

Weathering the Storm

A week before the start of my (Jeffrey M. Warren) first semester in academia, I sat down one evening at my desk in my home office. With a cup of hot tea in hand, my goal that evening was to develop a syllabus for an online crisis intervention course, and then create a full course shell using Blackboard, a learning management system (LMS) I was not extremely familiar with.

Four days later, I found myself mulling over the same syllabus. I was indecisive with everything! I even changed the syllabus font multiple times. What is more alarming is that I had yet to begin work on the course shell. What I had envisioned to be a piece of cake, was, in fact, no cakewalk.

Because the semester was drawing near, my inbox was inundated with emails from students, faculty, and others regarding scheduling issues, department meetings, and campus-wide events. I grew more and more stressed as my time was consumed by everything except prepping for this online course.

Two days before the start of fall classes, I changed my plan. Instead of prepping for the whole course, due to a self-imposed lack of time, I was forced to finalize the syllabus (whether I liked the font or not) and activate the course with only the first learning module completed. While this sounds like an agreeable consolation plan, what ensued was a semester of playing constant catch-up week to week while learning the ropes of higher education. I often procrastinated in developing and publishing the upcoming week's module, and I felt anxious when reading and responding to the students' discussion threads.

I frequently had fleeting notions that my students thought I was a fraud who had no clue what he was talking about. Fortunately, my end-of-semester instructor evaluations revealed that my students found the course rewarding and my efforts commendable. I had successfully weathered a 16-week storm. Regardless, I vowed never to fly by the seat of my pants again like I did with that course!

Checking In

1. How long does it take, or do you think it will take, for you to prepare for an online course?

2. What strategies do you use to reduce distractions during course preparation?

3. How do you manage stress during the semester?

4. How do you organize your schedule before, during, and after the semester?

5. Do your teaching evaluations typically align with your assessment of the quality of instruction?

The Overwrought Son

About a month before the beginning of a fall semester, Tony, a nontraditional student newly admitted to the program, contacted me via email to request the syllabus to a course he was scheduled to take. I didn't immediately respond to the eager lad since my schedule was clearly noted in the automatic out-of-office reply that he received. A day later, I received a voicemail message from the student followed by another email. I elected to respond via email and told him that I would disseminate the syllabus to the asynchronous online course on the first day of the semester, just as I typically do. I did not receive a reply from the student.

The first day of class arrived and at 8:34 a.m. that morning I received an email from Tony asking about the syllabus and access to the online course. I kindly let him know that the syllabus and course would be accessible at noon.

Throughout the semester, Tony emailed often to inquire about assignment rubrics, to request feedback, to ask to work ahead of schedule, and to seek clarification regarding due dates and deadlines. He also had minor dispositional and scheduling issues that arose when working on a group project that semester.

Tony completed the course, earning a B. Although he passed the course, I placed him on our departmental "watch list" as a student to monitor given the dispositional concerns. Other instructors and his advisor were surprised to hear of my concerns for Tony, indicating that he was a rather quiet, yet model student.

The following spring semester, I learned that Tony had been caring for his elderly mother (who later passed away) the semester he was in my class. Tony was under a lot of stress that semester, but he was uncomfortable disclosing personal issues to me or the class. These challenges, coupled with being a novice in online education, obviously led to responses atypical of his demeanor and prior performance. I was left wondering what I could have done differently to support Tony that semester.

Checking In

1. When do students typically receive the syllabus and access to the course?
2. Can students work ahead in other modules? If so, how far ahead?
3. Do students receive rubrics with clear expectations for all assignments?

4. How do students receive feedback?

5. How might students perceive your level of support and accessibility?

■ Allay Your Fears

Online instruction is not brand new, yet many have not fully embraced it as a replacement for brick-and-mortar education. The Internet is expansive; its full potential is largely unknown, especially within the helping professions. Though quite powerful, it can serve as a barrier to effective communication and instruction, leaving some participants wary, anxious, frustrated, and disengaged.

People prone to stress are likely to carry complicit thoughts and emotions into the online environment. For others, online learning may be a place of solace. The preceding scenarios are just a few examples of the ways in which students and instructors engage with technology and online learning. The following questionnaire supports your awareness of how your way of being translates to online learning and serves as a guide for further exploration and implementation of the fear-allaying strategies presented later in this chapter.

☐   I plan in advance and consistently follow a to-do list and calendar.

☐   Long-term goals for student learning are always in my purview.

☐   I often wait until the last minute to complete a task or project.

☐   When I am faced with adversity, I often retreat and delay responding to the situation.

☐   I believe that I have the ability to effectively teach in an online environment.

☐   I create welcoming and inviting learning communities inclusive of all students.

☐   I am an active participant in the process of learning in online environments.

☐   Students are empowered through, rather than dependent on, my instruction.

☐   I set realistic expectations for myself and my students.

☐   I take time to reflect on my day and make efforts to continually evolve professionally.

■ Strategies for Reducing Instructor Anxieties

As instructors, we meet the beginning of each semester with a range of emotions from excitement to dread. For some, teaching an online course adds an additional layer of joy, fear, or an emotion somewhere in between. In most cases, instructors persevere and manage with practical strategies to deliver the class. For others, these strategies are met with fierce resistance from the instructor's thoughts and emotions—these instructors need a more elegant solution.

Practical Strategies

Most online instructors have a pocket full of practical strategies they use to successfully deliver an online course. You can probably rattle off a few of your own go-to strategies for stress management. These strategies are typically behavioral and are easily observed by the students in your courses.

The acronym PACE (Prepare, Assert, Consistency, and Embrace technology) represents four key practical strategies. Online instructors who PACE themselves are poised to deliver an effective, stress-free curriculum.

Prepare

Online and hybrid instruction requires a different level of preparation than teaching in a face-to-face format. Instructors who plan in advance of the start of the semester are best positioned to minimize anxiety. By methodically developing a course, instructors can refine and retool throughout, making it a rewarding experience—one that will truly enthrall and enlighten students—rather than hastily throwing the course together with the bare minimum "nuts and bolts." Be bold, be daring, and bring on the bells and whistles!

Assert: Remain Present and Visible

Instructor presence and visibility are a key component of online instruction. By frequently asserting themselves in online courses, especially in asynchronous components, instructors send the message that they are invested in the process of learning. As a result, instructors build confidence, minimize stress, and display a level of control over the course that students are immediately privy to.

Developing an online presence fosters student investment and promotes accountability. It also allows instructors to be immediately aware of students who are struggling with concepts or interpersonal skills. Alternatively, when instructors are lackadaisical and infrequently check in on discussion threads and posts, there is more opportunity for problems to quickly spiral out of control. The longer the instructor refrains from actively engaging, the harder it is to become an active participant. In many cases, instructors rationalize not participating by telling themselves, "If I haven't heard from students, it must be going just fine." In some cases, instructors become anxious about what may be happening and therefore procrastinate even further.

Consistency

Online instructors who remain focused on the goal of providing effective instruction are more likely to behave in ways that support their aim, thereby minimizing anxiety and stress. When instructors waver and lack resolve, they become complacent and disengaged in the process. The result can be devastating to online classes and detrimental to the students enrolled.

Consistency involves organization, time management, and prioritization of tasks and responsibilities. It requires instructors who consistently and clearly articulate expectations, model professional dispositions, and adhere to the course syllabus minimize the opportunity for issues or problems to arise. The consistent instructor regularly posts announcements, timely and fairly grades assignments and exams, and releases new learning modules as outlined in the course syllabus.

Embrace Technology

Technology can be your best friend or your worst enemy. As we know, the time we invest in a friendship determines how strong the relationship is and the degree to which the friendship is reciprocated. The same applies to our "relationship" with technology. Online instructors must continually invest time in becoming well versed in the use of technology for course delivery. Best practices from 10 years ago—or even last year—are not likely the best practices of today. We cannot afford to have a distant relationship with technology if we intend to create a stress-free online instructional environment for ourselves and our students.

Commonly used education technology (LMSs, web conferencing platforms, and other instructional software) are frequently updated with new versions or "patches." Sometimes these updates alter our way of interacting with the technology just enough to create stress, especially if we are in the midst of instruction when we learn of the change. When you encounter an update or patch, pour yourself a cup of coffee and take a few minutes to acquaint yourself with the changes.

As you develop your course for the upcoming semester, go below the surface. Good friends connect on a deeper level. You've got to embrace the good, the bad, and the ugly, and this means recognizing that videos and links change and break. Putting in time up front to check for broken links to course content can save time and minimize stress later. It will also reduce the clutter in your inbox from confused students, which is something that we all strive for.

An Elegant Strategy

While the practical strategies noted so far in this chapter can certainly help to reduce or thwart stress and anxiety, sometimes a different type of solution is needed. As a member of the helping professions, you are probably familiar with rational emotive and cognitive behavioral therapy (RE-CBT). RE-CBT evolved in the 1960s from the work of psychology pioneers including Albert Ellis and Tim Beck. Borrowing from Stoic philosophy, they suggested that people are not disturbed by things but by the views taken of those things. When rigid or demanding thoughts (also known as irrational thoughts) are maintained, feelings such as anger, anxiety, and stress emerge. These emotions typically lead to unhelpful behaviors that can have a detrimental impact on professional obligations. For example, an online instructor may have a solid plan to prepare online course shells in advance of the semester start. Although a plan is in place, the instructor also thinks these tasks will be too difficult for her to complete, especially during the winter break. She believes she shouldn't have to spend time working on this during break and that doing so would be terrible. These irrational thoughts lead the instructor to procrastinate, feel bad about procrastinating, and then experience anxiety and stress due to a lack of preparedness.

RE-CBT provides a viable framework and tools for instructors to address irrational thoughts that impede their success. The ABC model of emotional disturbance is a great resource instructors can use to become more aware of their thoughts, feelings, and behaviors.

We continue with this example in the applied ABC model offered in the following section. Additional information on the ABC model is available by searching for "REBT Self-help Form" in your web browser.

ABC Model of Emotional Disturbance

Antecedent: Make a plan to develop course shells between fall and spring semesters.

Beliefs: "I shouldn't have to exert this amount of energy over the break."

Consequences:

- Cognitive: "I never have time to do what I want in between the semesters."
- Emotional: Anxiety/anger.
- Behavioral: Procrastination.

Disputations: "Is it the end of the world that I have to do a little work over the break? Furthermore, is it really that difficult a task considering the work some people are doing at the moment?"

Effective Rational Belief: "It's a lot of work but I can handle it. I'm fortunate to have time off; working on it now is better than working on it while in the throes of a busy semester."

Functional Emotions/Behaviors: Slight annoyance while working to develop the online course shell.

Goal Reached: Completion of the task a week prior to the start of the semester.

This model can be highly effective for instructors who experience unhealthy negative emotions that impede their ability to instruct and support students. Instructors may have the very best intentions; however, they become derailed by their own cognitions. Instructors who understand and incorporate this model can enhance their instruction and model healthy thoughts, feelings, and behaviors to their students.

Strategies for Supporting Anxious Students

Students have common expectations when enrolled in face-to-face courses: attend class on designated days and times, sit at a table or desk, receive a lecture, take notes, participate in a group activity, and be dismissed from the class. However, online learning may not have a common expectation because the experience varies depending on the degree of course synchronization, student work space options, student competence in technology navigation, computer literacy of students and instructor, Internet gremlins, and Internet access in general. With these additional variables at play, it is obvious that online instruction can heighten emotions for instructors and students. Instructors can take steps to reduce potentially stressful situations. The acronym CARE, which stands for Community of learners, Attend to the details, Reinforce, and Engagement, describes key strategies instructors can use to reduce stress and anxiety among students.

Community of Learners

Online learning can be a lonely endeavor. Students with extroverted personalities may experience frustration as a result of this loneliness. In contrast, introverted students may be content with little or no interaction, and too much interaction could be stressful.

For online instructors, it is important to build a sense of community (Song, Singleton, Hill, & Koh, 2004, pp. 59–70) that is learner-centered and meets the needs of all students (Smith, 2005, pp. 1–18). Anxiety related to online learning is significantly related to course satisfaction (Bolliger & Halupa, 2012, pp. 81–98), so instructors should consider methods that increase satisfaction through student orientation, student-centered approaches, and intentional interventions. Also, online instructors who develop learner-centered communities demonstrate authenticity and genuineness similar to person-centered counseling, thus alleviating stress and anxiety (Rogers, 1951).

Attend to Detail

On occasion, even the most detail-oriented person lacks detail. In the same vein, a great communicator may at times fail to communicate. As I'm sure you know, the meaning or message behind a comment may be perceived in different, and often unintended, ways. Because online instruction occurs through a virtual medium, there is even greater potential for meaning to be "lost in translation." Because online learning presents barriers for some students, they may be less likely to ask questions for clarification, and these same students may also grapple with the nuances of technology all alone.

It is important for the instructor to be as detailed as possible when conveying instructions, expectations, and feedback, though we often find ourselves on autopilot. We copy and paste feedback on student assignments, recycle old course announcements, fail to revise assignment descriptions on syllabi that created confusion the previous semester, and cringe at the thought of returning a student's phone call. These instructors may save a bit of time, yet provoke stress and anxiety among students each semester because they do not attend to the details. In the end, this tradeoff (i.e., time for stress) benefits no one and hinders the learning process.

Reinforce: Offer Ongoing Support

Students sometimes need to be reminded that they have the tools for success. A few years ago, I served as the director of a graduate program. Each year, during admission interviews I would tell applicants that if they were admitted, I believed that they had the tools to be successful in our program and as professionals who would change the lives of the clients they worked with. I was planting a seed that I would later water (reinforce) and watch grow as students matriculated through the program. Students who were thus empowered were often more resilient and less stressed when faced with adversity. They knew I believed in them, and sometimes that was the deciding factor between persevering and giving up.

It is important that we foster conditions that support and empower students. Spending time getting to know students gives instructors the opportunity to understand student strengths and limitations. As a result, instructors can offer individualized support.

Reinforcing unconditional support inherently thwarts stress and anxiety and promotes determination and growth. However, online instructors must be cautious about not encouraging dependency by providing excessive support. For example, instructors can direct students to a tutorial for uploading assignments to the LMS rather than accepting the assignment via email. This strategy promotes independence while helping the student build confidence in navigating the world of online education.

Engagement

It is challenging for people to experience multiple diverging emotions simultaneously. It behooves instructors to use strategies that excite and engage students. If used intentionally and methodically, differentiated instruction can lead toward excitement, growth, and student engagement. For example, an instructor of a micro-skills course may use scaffolding (see Chapter 8 for information on scaffolding) to teach a set of basic helping skills (e.g., paraphrasing, summarizing). After viewing a brief video-recorded lecture and reading verbatim session transcripts, students watch a mock demonstration and are asked to respond to five prompts by using these skills. Students also practice the skills with a family member or friend. During the weekly synchronous class session, students break out into small groups to practice the micro-skills further, prior to a large group interactive discussion of student experiences. The lesson concluded with a check-in quiz (St. Clair, 2015, p. 129). This instructional plan allows for guided practice and independent practice with prompt feedback, which reduces student frustration and fosters engagement (Hara & Kling, 2000, pp. 557–579).

Online instructors should also consider using tools and resources that help students connect course content to the "real world." You may still wonder what the purpose was of that calculus course you took in high school, but if your teacher had shown you how it applied to everyday life, it would have piqued your interest. At a minimum, your heart would not race as you reflect on that calculus exam.

■ Takeaways

The strategies offered in this chapter are not exhaustive, yet should serve as a platform for exploring strategies to allay fear and anxiety. Practical strategies such as PACE and the ABC Model are good options for instructors seeking solace regarding unmanageable stress. Finally, instructors must demonstrate they CARE if students are to succeed and experience online learning for what it truly is: a viable vehicle to accessible education.

HELPFUL TIP: In academia, stress is imminent! Stress can help us move forward, but it can also paralyze. Take time to practice self-care and encourage your students to do the same. Consider the perspectives of your students and remember that things are never as bad as they seem.

"Clear your mind of CAN'T."—Unknown

Resources

Hailey, D. E., Grant-Davie, K., & Hult, C. A. (2001). Online education horror stories worthy of Halloween: A short list of problems and solutions in online instruction. *Computers and Composition, 18*(4), 387–397. doi:10.1016/S8755-4615(01)00070-6

References

Bolliger, D. U., & Halupa, C. (2012). Student perceptions of satisfaction and anxiety in an online doctoral program. *Distance Education, 33*(1), 81–98. doi:10.1080/01587919.2012.667961

Hara, N., & Kling, R. (2000). Student distress in a web-based distance education course. *Information, Communication & Society, 3*(4), 557–579. doi:10.1080/13691180010002297

Rogers, C. R. (1951). *Client-centered therapy.* Boston, MA: Houghton Mifflin. Retrieved from https://www.positivepsychologyprogram.com/client-centered-therapy

Smith, T. C. (2005). Fifty-one competencies for online instruction. *Journal of Educators Online, 2*(2), 1–18. doi:10.9743/JEO.2005.2.2

Song, L., Singleton, E. S., Hill, J. R., & Koh, M. H. (2004). Improving online learning: Student perceptions of useful and challenging characteristics. *The Internet and Higher Education, 7*(1), 59–70. doi:10.1016/j.iheduc.2003.11.003

St. Clair, D. A. (2015). Simple suggestion for reducing first-time online student anxiety. *Journal of Online Learning and Teaching, 11*(1), 129. Retrieved from http://jolt.merlot.org/vol11no1/StClair_0315.pdf

CHAPTER 4

Meeting Students Where They Are At: Staying Student Focused

In this chapter, we focus on the student voice: their thoughts, experiences, and expectations. The student voice is important to consider when developing and teaching course content. To glean this information, we asked several students studying helping professions online to answer questions about their experience in the online environment. Learning from students about their preferences and how they individually and collectively engage with the technology and content is helpful as you prepare your course; making your course a student-centered one improves both student success and course/program outcomes.

OVERARCHING QUESTIONS

1. How can online instructors effectively meet the needs of students?
2. What suggestions would students offer faculty who are developing online courses?
3. What information would be beneficial for a new online learner to know before, during, and after taking an online course?
4. What did you enjoy and learn from your online learning experience?
5. As a student, what advice would you give to new online instructors as they begin to develop their course(s)?
6. What advice would you give to students considering a course of online study?

■ Guided Prompts

Describe three characteristics of your student population (e.g., demographics, learning style, comfort level with technology):

1. _____

2. _____

3. _____

Consider the region and location where you live and teach. What factors might you need to consider about your audience and the type of student your institution draws? For example, do you draw from a rural or urban population? How diverse is your region? Do your students work or attend classes full-time? Are students taking one course, a nondegree program, a degree-seeking program, or another plan of study? Meeting the students "where they are at" collectively and individually is essential.

VIGNETTE

In rural North Carolina, Linda, a mother of two young children, has just started to think about taking a few human development classes. She is fascinated by human interaction and her friends tell her to consider social work as a profession because she is such an amazing listener.

Linda works full-time as an administrative analyst at a technology company, but she wants to continue her education and to model lifelong learning to her children. As appealing as it is for her to dream about changing careers, she struggles to figure out how to attend classes without leaving work and how she will fit one more thing into her busy life.

After she puts her kids to bed, Linda sits down at her makeshift desk and Googles "social work programs in NC." She is surprised that there are social work classes, and even complete master's degree-level programs offered online. She hasn't taken a college class in 10 years and has never taken an online course before. She looks up from her computer to ponder this for a minute and notices a pile of blue Legos, a stack of paperwork yet to be tackled, and part of a dried-out orange peel sitting on the desk by her computer. She sighs.

It is decision time for Linda. Will she clean up the desk now or take a few minutes to learn about social work programs? She tries to envision her life 20 years down the road, and then she gets intentional. With a grand sweep, Linda brushes the orange peel into the garbage can and begins reading about the online program. The thought of taking classes, especially online classes, makes her feel a little nervous, and she has a bunch of questions. She wonders:

- Will I feel connected to my instructor and classmates in online courses?

- Is it possible to learn online content that is so personal and relational?

- Can classes in counseling, human development, and the helping professions really be taught effectively online?

- Do I have the technological skills to manage an online learning system?

- Do I have the time, space, and finances to make this happen?

- How will I integrate my family, professional career, and academic work simultaneously to achieve this goal toward obtaining a master's degree in social work?

The advantages of online courses are intriguing to her, though. She can attend classes from home so she will not have to leave her children or find child care, and she doesn't have to drive to campus and pay for parking. The flexibility of an online program would allow her to integrate school with her work schedule and family life.

In a burst of hopeful anticipation, Linda clicks the button to make an appointment to speak with the admissions office about applying for the program.

This student vignette highlights a realistic entry point of the prospective online student. As online instructors, it is important for us to recognize the varied experiences of our students and the unique situations each student brings to the classroom. For some students, working full or part-time is part of their world. Many students are concurrently raising children, supporting parents, taking care of pets, and participating in other important aspects of daily life.

Instructors and administrators spend extreme amounts of time planning and developing programs and courses, and in great courses, students remain at the epicenter of course design as content is developed. Because student experiences and learning outcomes are critical, it is vitally important to ask them about their specific needs coming into the program. Their reactions and feedback during the experience and evaluation after the class and/or program ends are valuable information too.

We sent a questionnaire to online students across disciplines within the helping professions to gather information about their experience: what worked, what didn't work, what helped them to feel engaged in the learning process, what bored them, and so on. Quotes from these students are interspersed throughout the chapter to punctuate and personalize important lessons for prospective online instructors.

Before we review the student voices, let's take a look at how students learn and the theory about learning.

■ Learning Theory

There are, generally, three styles of learning: visual, auditory, and tactile. This means that most of us learn by watching, listening, or doing. Most students use a combination of styles, with one style dominant. As instructors (regardless of the type of class), it is important that we present material in a way that will address the needs of all three types of learners. However, for online instructors, it is important to provide content in multiple formats, because connecting the content to the student is essential.

Visual learners remember material with images that can be grasped by sight. These students are easily distracted by simple audio files that do not include visual cues. Auditory learners absorb spoken material, so verbal instruction resonates with these learners. For them, consider creating "voice-overs" or audio files that explain assignments. Finally, tactile learners are "hands on." These students enjoy learning when it includes a physical component. They learn by doing, where they can touch, move, draw, or build. Due to the lack of interaction in asynchronous environments, this type of learner may be the hardest to engage. However, having activities that involve clicking a mouse or using touch-pad technology may be particularly helpful for these learners. Consider offering opportunities for students to build a matrix, genogram, Lucid chart, or the like.

It is also important for instructors to understand their own inclinations and styles. Remember that just because one style is your preferred learning method doesn't mean it will resonate with your students. Self-awareness is key here. Instructors can have students take a self-assessment and discuss or upload the results. An online search of the term "learning style self-assessment" will provide several options for online quizzes that can be assigned to students. Instructors can also complete self-assessments to learn more about their own preferred learning and teaching styles to help them teach a full range of learner types.

Questions for the Instructor's Consideration:

1. As I prepare and plan for my course, what key points do I want my students to leave the class knowing?

2. Are there ways to assess students' learning throughout the course to ensure that my plan is on track and the message is received as I intended? In what ways can I measure student success in my course?

3. What do I hope students retain from the course and/or program?

4. What student comments would put a smile on my face while reading my student evaluation?

5. After the course is over, the one specific comment about my course from my students that I would enjoy reading is: _____.

As online programs and courses are developed and offered, what characteristics of the online environment do students appreciate and learn the most from throughout their coursework and/or program?

Characteristics of the online environment can relate to how the content is delivered via a learning management system (LMS) (i.e., asynchronously), synchronously (i.e., meeting virtually at the same time, date, and link), hybrid classes, and blended learning environments (i.e., a combination of online and virtual environments). Additionally, the students' preferred learning style may come into play as they share their most favored ways to learn content and engage with the instructors.

■ Understanding Student Voices

We asked students a set of questions to glean from them the essence of the online learner's experience. We wanted to know why they chose online in lieu of on-campus classes, what they appreciated and didn't appreciate about the online environment and course design, and what advice they would offer to novice online students and instructors. In general, the demographics of the students are: age 20 to 65; diverse ethnicities and races, including Caucasian, African American, Asian American, nontraditional, male and female; and graduate students from rural and urban locations in the Southeast.

Here are the results.

Why Did You Choose Courses or Programs Offered Online in Lieu of on Campus?

"I was working part-time, and the flexible online format allowed me to learn on my own schedule without in-class attendance required . . . it cut down on the number of weekly trips I had to make to campus."

"I loved the flexibility of online learning in conjunction with a part-time job, no travel, and accessing infinite resources beyond the textbook."

"I decided to take classes online because of its convenience. I work full-time, and I really wanted to continue my education without losing my financial security."

Takeaway: Online learning is expanding the norm of the traditional student who is under 22 years old, a full-time student, and lives near campus. Many people who register for online classes and programs are already in the middle of a career, are raising children, and have family and community duties at night and on the weekend. This is not to say that courses should be made less rigorous to fit student needs, but thoughtful consideration of course design (e.g., specific, concrete due dates versus floating due dates) can make these programs more compatible with all students' needs.

What Were Your Concerns About Online Courses and Programs?

"I was worried about how effective the classes would be. I really didn't want to sign up for something that requires reading the textbook, posting comments, and taking an exam. That is so boring and really wouldn't have taught me much."

"My previous experiences made me think of online learning as very isolated and individualized with little to no interaction with classmates."

Takeaway: A personal relationship between student and instructor and between students is vitally important to online learners. Instructors must be intentional about carving out spaces for these relationships to flourish. Students appreciate a personal touch from the instructor even before the semester begins. Instructors send welcome letters to students a week or two before the semester begins to invite the students into a relationship; a letter like this will be a big step toward reducing uncertainty with new students and begin to build rapport. The letter may highlight the structure of the course and give details about the requisite technology and other course information. A personal touch and connection early on are essential to a successful and productive semester.

Also, online course content should be dynamic. Simply having students read and respond to discussion posts or forums may not meet the learning needs of students. It is important to have multiple modes of providing instruction. Assigning interactive quizzes, assessments, and activities will reduce boredom and increase the interaction with the course material, thereby effectively conveying course concepts.

What Challenges Did You Experience as a Novice Online Learner?

"On the rare times I encountered technical difficulties, my lack of background caused a bit of anxiety, but the situations always managed to get resolved swiftly."

"The only thing I didn't like about online learning was the uncertainty with the technology."

". . . it was a challenge if the platform or students' individual computer systems weren't working appropriately."

"Online learning requires a little more self-discipline . . ."

"I did miss the opportunity to meet classmates and faculty in person."

"It was more of a challenge to remember and prioritize the online courses."

"By being on the computer, it is so much easier to zone out and get distracted than if you were in a classroom."

Takeaway: Technology, time management, self-management, and instructor–student relationships were the top concerns of the online students we questioned. Instructors can assist students with these issues and others as well as improve the course design via the use of assessment tools. Regular assessments allow you to check in with students throughout the course to evaluate their experience and how they are feeling about the technology, online environment, content, and so on. For the instructor, creating a framework for hearing your student voices throughout the semester is imperative.

By identifying a process and method for soliciting input and feedback about the student experience, you can support learning outcomes and goals as well as your effectiveness as an instructor. In most cases, feedback is offered toward the end of the semester as an end-of-semester evaluation. However, we can encourage and provide multiple touch points and opportunities for students to share their experience throughout the semester. For example, in an online synchronous environment, we can ask students to anonymously write on the whiteboard:

- A learning point, structure, or process that instructors should continue
- A "muddy" point that should be addressed or is confusing for the student
- A suggestion on ways to adapt and change areas that may be confusing or more informative or helpful for the student learning outcomes

Engaging students as part of the process will inadvertently help them to be more invested in their own learning and experience. The goal is for students to be active agents in their learning process and provide multiple points in time throughout the semester to provide feedback and discussion.

It can be scary to put yourself out there in this way, by asking for review of your work thus far. However, you may be surprised to learn that not all the feedback will be negative. We suggest framing this evaluation as an opportunity and using their feedback as valuable information to improve and enhance your course as well as the overall experience for the students. Keep in mind student anonymity in this process and remind them that their feedback and suggestions will in no way affect their grades in the course.

WORD TO THE WISE: If and when you ask for feedback, consider how you are going to use it and disperse the information to the students. For example, will you summarize the comments and develop action steps for feedback that require change? One of the frustrations from students is when we ask for feedback and they spend the time sharing their thoughts, but nothing changes and/or the information and results are not shared and acted upon within the class or expeditiously after the feedback is given. Acknowledging to students when we are unable to make the changes quickly or within the semester is also important in developing and sustaining rapport. For example, if an assignment was given and students report that the points were unclear or not specific, it may be too late to revamp this assignment for this semester. However, validating that their concerns were heard and taken into consideration is an important next step. Then, offering alternatives and ways to adapt future assignments demonstrates through concrete actions that you have heard their concerns and are willing to adapt based on their feedback and suggestions.

As you progress through the semester, you may ask yourself these reflective questions:

1. What do you know about your students?
2. How can you get to know them better?
3. What challenges are students facing with on-campus and online instruction or programs, specifically courses offered in the helping professions?
4. How can you, as the instructor, address and mediate any challenges?
5. What are a few concrete steps to take to get to know your students?

What Did You Find Helpful About the Design of Your Online Course?

"I enjoyed the courses that used both Moodle (asynchronous) and Blackboard (synchronous) platforms as they allowed me to get to know my classmates and professor better."

"What I thought was really cool was that we had the capability to do everything that is typically done in the classroom."

"I liked being able to 'meet' weekly with my classmates and participate in discussion and tasks outside of the [independent study] completing online prompts and reflections."

"I was pleasantly surprised to discover that I was able to handle the technology, and the institutions' technology provided only minimal technical difficulties."

"I do appreciate that each class session was recorded, which does allow you to review what you may have missed . . ."

"Online classes taught with synchronous and asynchronous far exceeded my expectations and allowed me to feel as though the class was taught in person . . ."

"Most of my online classes were a combination of synchronous and asynchronous. I have also taken an asynchronous-only course. My preference is definitely the combination format."

"Synchronous learning is important for skill practice and development allowing for learners to practice skills with and on each other."

Takeaway: Interactivity is where it's at for students. Gone are the days when online classes were independent studies. This is especially true for classes in the helping professions, as instructors serve as role models, and what we teach is key to future professional success for the students.

Also, completely asynchronous classes are a bit challenging for students. Although they offer extensive flexibility, they may not meet student needs for community and content. If it is not practical or feasible to offer a hybrid course, consider having "optional" synchronous engagement with students. Provide option opportunities for students to gather in an online group at a particular time. For students who need the additional interaction, it will meet their needs while not requiring it for students who have less forgiving schedules.

In What Way Did Online Class Design Work Better for You Than On-Campus Classes?

"In a way, my online classes were a little better than a face-to-face class as I felt more comfortable expressing myself. I didn't have to worry about having all eyes on me when I spoke."

"As one who thinks long before speaking, especially when learning, I enjoyed more thorough participation in discussion boards than a real-time class situation would ordinarily afford me."

"The faculty-led discussions were focused, such that tangents or dominant personalities were less likely to derail the learning process."

Takeaway: Online courses provide a distinct advantage over on-campus classes for some types of personalities—the reserved, quiet, and slow-to-speak students. A well-designed online environment can create a space for greater class participation and student input, and an instructor can facilitate this by actively engaging (or disengaging) with particular students.

Did You Discover Any Personal or Professional Advantages to Learning to Navigate Online Platforms and Environments Beyond Success in the Classroom?

"I enjoyed learning to use the technology and becoming more comfortable with presenting information in an online-compatible format."

"Learning in this way can also help open people's minds to the idea of receiving assistance and help through various methods if they aren't open to physically meeting with a counselor/therapist in person."

"Introducing students to the ethics of technology used in the helping professions is critical, with continued expansion of technology used in these professions."

Takeaway: The future of the helping professions is going to include online professional service and engagement. It is important that tomorrow's helping professionals learn to feel comfortable in online environments and with the technology. Also, properly modeling behavior, ethics, relationships, and personal awareness while online emphasizes a distinct skill that modern students need to learn.

What Advice Would You Offer to Novice Online Students?

"Make sure your computer is as up to date as possible with needed technology."

"Ask questions in class or to your professor if you have issues with your technology or the platforms."

"Get familiar with logging on way before the semester starts."

"Test out the features of the platform when you get a chance."

"Consider whether you have the internal motivation and discipline to embark on an online learning journey, since there isn't face-to-face encouragement to keep up from faculty."

"Enter fully into the discussions, assignments, etc. to gain the most from the experience . . . [. T]here was a surprising depth of discussion among learners that I would have missed had I not chosen to fully engage."

"Be open to the online platforms and know that you can get a similar experience as an on-campus course if the appropriate energy and outlook is applied . . ."

Takeaway: This is great advice! If you send a pre-course welcome letter, it is a great idea to encourage your students to get familiar with platforms and technology you will be using for the course. It is also important for novice online instructors to spend time in their online environment testing out features and gauging how much time activities and class assignments require. It will be helpful to remember that some of your students will be novices to online learning and perhaps they may thus need a little more guidance and grace than usually required in on-campus classes. For online programs, offering an orientation prior to the beginning of class provides a way for students to meet and instructors to cover the technology and expectations of the courses. Additionally, orientation to the program, either in person or virtually, can begin the rapport and community-building process before students enter their first class. Orientation can allay some of the fears of incoming students.

What Advice Would You Offer to Novice Online Instructors and Course Developers?

"In order for students to get the most out of the course, the professor must be competent and knowledgeable in best practices for online learning."

"Make the experience as engaging as possible. . . . For some topics, lectures may be needed, but don't lecture the whole class period."

"I had a GREAT experience with online learning because my courses were taught by wonderfully responsive educators who crafted excellent learning opportunities."

"It is best if online courses are as interactive as possible. Please include such activities as polls, videos, group presentations, and small group discussions."

"Courses that just used Moodle (asynchronous) fell below my expectations."

"Professors must be competent and knowledgeable in best practices for online learning."

"[One instructor] did an amazing job of teaching the online courses I took . . . . Although we never saw her face-to-face, we felt connected to her and the rest of our classmates."

"Professors should consider allowing discussions between students through synchronous learning and including small group discussions/ tasks."

"Ensure that all up-to-date technology and support are available."

Takeaway: The students we surveyed strongly preferred courses that were designed to combine synchronous and asynchronous platforms. The students enjoyed the structure and organization provided by the asynchronous platforms and the interactivity and relationship-building capacity of synchronous platforms. Instructors can boost their relationships with students by building in time to connect with them in "real time," such as offering virtual office hours. Hosting attendance-optional meetings from time to time to share ideas, discuss a question, and so on, is also a good relational model.

Students also enjoyed and learned more from instructors who felt comfortable and were competent with their course design and the online environment. When it comes to the technology and learning platforms, winging it is not an option!

■ Guided Reflection

Based on what you already know about your student population and their needs, what are three specific tasks you can complete to prepare for the semester to run smoothly? (e.g., connecting with the disability services office, working with the office of technology to ensure accessibility of content for all students, preparing content to address any gaps in student experiences).

1. _____
2. _____
3. _____

If you have taught in the past, more than likely you have received feedback from students through formal or informal evaluations. Review and reflect on the evaluations as you prepare to teach the next course. Identify the course you will be teaching next. List three areas of growth and/or challenges you hope to address in the next semester of teaching this course to support student learning outcomes.

1. _____
2. _____
3. _____

HELPFUL TIP: Students appreciate preparation and a personal touch from the instructor, even before the semester begins. Instructors can offer a welcome letter to students a week or two before the semester begins, which highlights the structure of the course, details with regard to technology, and other important information. A personal touch and connection early on are essential to a successful and productive semester. For example, adding your favorite quotes or poem to the end of your announcements or emails can personalize your communication with your students and make you more relatable.

> *"Give a man a fish and you feed him for a day; teach a man to fish and you feed him for a lifetime."—Maimonides*

Authors' Note

The authors would like to thank the students who provided such valuable reflections about their experiences to this chapter. Specific former students we would like to acknowledge Cyhthia Broderius, Jodi Brown, Gabrielle Denise Jones, Jessica L. Oxendine, Susan H. Ward, and many others who are not noted here. Without amazing students like the ones mentioned here, our work and this book would not be possible.

CHAPTER 5

Drawing From the Research: A Cursory Overview

VIGNETTE

It was a daunting task for new counseling professor, Dr. O'Brien, to teach an online counseling skills class in the coming semester. He had just started teaching a year earlier at a small public university in the southeast United States. There was little technical support for him on his campus and no other professors in his department had taught online before. He had taken one or two classes with Moodle when he was a counseling student, but he knew little about online teaching. The first thing he thought he should do was study the research information about online teaching and learning. He hoped to find something useful in the literature about online instruction that would benefit him and his students.

OVERARCHING QUESTIONS

1. What do we know about online teaching and student learning in the helping professions?
2. What are the ethical considerations for online teaching?
3. How should we teach clinical skills and supervision online?

If you are going to design and teach an online course, you want to give it your best shot, right? We have reviewed the current literature and best practices from online learning programs across the country and current research in the helping professions, including counseling, social work, and psychology. The following research information gives us insight into creating the most effective programs/courses for the best student outcomes.

■ Early Studies

Early research studies found no significant differences in effectiveness between distance education and face-to-face education, suggesting that distance education can successfully replace face-to-face instruction (Bernard et al., 2004; Cavanaugh, 2001; Moore, 1994). Individual studies of job-related courses comparing web-based and classroom-based learning indicate that online learning is superior to classroom-based instruction (Sitzmann, Kraiger, Stewart, & Wisher, 2006; Wisher & Olson, 2003). However, researchers generally concluded that online and face-to-face courses resulted in essentially similar learning among students.

In 2010, the U.S. Department of Education published a national comprehensive study on online education (Means, Toyama, Murphy, Bakia, & Jones, 2010). It is a meta-analysis on 50 individual studies from 1996–2008; 43 studies were about adults (undergraduates or older) and seven studies were in Grades K–12. (The methodology of the study can be found at the end of this chapter.) Here are the conclusions of the study.

Is Online Learning Better Than Face-to-Face Classes?

Among the 50 individual studies contrast between online and face-to-face instruction, 11 students significantly favored the online or blended learning course. The study reveals that instruction conducted entirely online is as effective as classroom instruction, but no better. Blending of online and face-to-face instruction, on average, had stronger learning outcomes than either face-to-face instruction alone or online-only instruction.

What Practices Are Associated With Effective Online Learning?

The variables of pedagogy/learning experience, computer-mediated communication with instructor, computer-mediated communication with peers, class length, media features, time on task, one-way video or audio, computer-based instruction elements, opportunity for face-to-face time with instructor, opportunity for face-to-face time with peers, opportunity to practice, and feedback provided were weighed with respect to efficacy of learning. Only collaborative instruction and instructor-directed instruction were found to be positively related to effective online learning.

What Conditions or Learner Types Fare Best in Online Classrooms?

Three subsets of learner types were studied: K–12 students, undergraduate students (the largest single group), and other students (graduate students or individuals receiving job-related training). The study covered a range of professions, though medicine and health care were the most common. These studies were contrasted with studies in other fields regarding the following question: What conditions influence the effectiveness of online learning? No significant differences were found. The study shows that for the range of student types for which studies are available, the effectiveness of online learning was equivalent in older and newer studies for K–12, undergraduate, and older learners and in both medical and other subject areas.

Did the Research Method Affect the Results?

Comparisons of the three designs of the research studies (random-assignment experiments, quasi-experiments with statistical control, and crossover designs) indicate that study design is not significant as a moderator variable.

Effect sizes were larger for studies in which the online and face-to-face conditions varied in terms of curriculum materials, instructional approach, and the medium of instruction.

A major limitation of this study is that the conditions varied among the 50 contrasts:

- Analysts could document the use of one-way video or audio for only 14 effects
- 16 contrasts involved only asynchronous communication between student and instructor
- 8 allowed both asynchronous and synchronous online communication
- 26 contrasts came from studies that did not document the types of online communication provided between the instructor and learners

The U.S. Department of Education's study also reviewed experimental and quasi-experimental studies contrasting various online learning practices. These are the conclusions of the review:

- Online-only and combination classes implemented within a single study demonstrated similar student learning outcomes in both settings.
- Unique multimedia functions offered in most learning management systems do not appear to influence the amount that students learn in online classes. For example, videos do not appear to enhance learning and online quizzes do not seem to be more effective than other tactics, such as assigning homework.
- Giving students control over their use of offered media and prompting student reflection enhance learning. Student activity, reflection, and self-monitoring boost positive outcomes.
- Support mechanisms, such as guiding questions, influence how students interact together in an online classroom, but they do not influence how much students learn.

Some researchers have suggested that this pattern may change, arguing that online learning as practiced in the 21st century, including synchronous and asynchronous learning modes, can be expected to outperform earlier forms of distance education in terms of effects on learning (Zhao, Lei, Yan, Lai, & Tan, 2005).

▪ Online Learning in Helping Professions Education

There is not a lot of research into helping profession education and online learning. However, in 2015, a group of researchers examined online and face-to-face graduate level counselor education students (Smith et al., 2015). Similar gains in learning were found in both groups; however, the students in the online group favored online instruction for perceived learning efficiency. This may have occurred because the professor initiated more interactions with online learners than with face-to-face learners.

Student Response and Satisfaction

One study on online teaching in counseling looked at facilitative factors. The findings show that instructor characteristics are important: frequency of participation in discussion forums, constructive and positive feedback to students, and quick return of assignments. The personal characteristics of students are also important (e.g., motive for taking the course, discipline, and time management skills; Ekong, 2006).

Student satisfaction is frequently the focus of research studies. One research study examined student satisfaction factors in graduate distance education in counseling programs (Palmer & McBride, 2012). Student satisfaction factors include student factors (lifestyle commitments, learning styles, student motivation, and task value and self-efficacy), faculty factors (faculty knowledge and experience, instructor feedback style, instructor accessibility to students, and instructor interactions with students), course factors (course content and course structure), community interactions (social networking and support, peer-influenced learning), and support systems factors (technological access and ability, technological and administrative support).

A study conducted on an online counseling theory class examined whether students in an online class performed the same on weekly quizzes as students in a traditional classroom and whether student satisfaction with the course instructor differed from their on-campus peers (Lyke & Frank, 2012). Results show no significant differences between the scores of the two groups on the weekly quizzes, but students in the online class were less satisfied with the course and with instruction overall. However, there was little information about the curriculum or instruction. Based on the limited information from the article, it appears that the online class was asynchronous only (Ting, 2016).

Program Planning and Design

In 2005, researchers looked at three universities in western Canada that offered predominantly online Master of Counseling programs (Collins & Jerry, 2005[1]). The programs are part-time and take 3 years to complete.

In the design of the curriculum, administrators ensured that the online program reflected the standardization of the curriculum. Outcome competencies for the overall program were mapped onto specific courses to ensure that each student grasped the core competency set. There was also a comprehensive competency matrix for the curriculum that allows students to link competency development and curriculum throughout the program. Next, the administrators developed means to measure the overall competency foundation: learning objectives, interactive web-based learning objects and activities, online discussion forum topics for each course, and online course evaluations.

In the design of course assignments, the instructors mapped onto Bloom's taxonomy of educational objectives to reflect the knowledge, affective, and skills domains targeted in the overall competency framework and to provide clear criteria for grading in each area.

Counseling is an applied practice program, so it is important that all courses emphasize the application of knowledge to practice as well as the development of professionally relevant attitudes and beliefs. These three online programs link the course objectives to professional practice competencies, including experiential and reflective activities. The students are challenged to address personal biases and attitudinal barriers and integrate their learning and personal values.

In online learning for helping professions, such as counseling, communication between the instructor and the students as well as among the students is preferred and seems to be most valued by the students (Ting, 2016).

▪ Ethical Issues

In counselor education, the Council for Accreditation of Counseling and Related Educational Programs (CACREP) guides counselor education practices. The CACREP 2009 Standards state, "Evidence exists of the use and infusion of technology in program delivery and technology's impact on the counseling profession" (CACREP, 2008). However, the findings on this topic are inconclusive owing to the limited number of research studies and small sample size (Clingerman & Bernard, 2004).

---

[1] This article reports the basic structure of the program; the web-based delivery system; communication tools employed; and the philosophical, pedagogical, programmatic, and administrative principles and concepts foundation for development and implementation.

Online education is nascent, especially in the helping professions, and little evidence of effectiveness was found in the literature about the impact of online learning in counselor education.

Confidentiality in online learning is an ethical concern, and it may prevent counselor educators from adopting teaching technologies as rapidly as educators in some other fields (Krieger & Stockton, 2004). However, technology is advancing and new technology and software will arise to cover the issues of privacy and confidentiality. (For more information on ethics, see Chapter 11.)

Issues of self-care are another ethical concern. Is it suitable to cover self-care in a fully online counseling program (Krieger & Stockton, 2004)? A few researchers examined the connection between perceived wellness and current well-being of counseling students in an online course (Merryman, Martin, & Martin, 2015, p. 3). One hundred online students from two small colleges were surveyed online with the Scales of Psychological Well-Being and Perceived Wellness. The findings show that 64% of students had participated in individual counseling, and of these, 89% found the counseling to be beneficial. Of the students surveyed, 53% had sought counseling on their own. However, participation in personal counseling was not significantly correlated with personal wellness. Overall psychological well-being positively correlated with perceived wellness, including perceived wellness as a purpose in life. Psychological well-being accounted for 80% of the variance in relation to perceived wellness, which indicates that online students are capable of recognizing their state of mental health. The results suggest that students are most helped by general well-being and a sense of meaning or purpose. The findings may provide a way to evaluate the well-being of distance education students, which may provide an answer to the concern about suitability for online counseling education. Also, this study suggests that students' self-report of their own well-being provides an accurate measure of their wellness. This offers support for teaching counseling via the online format and for trusting the online students' autonomy for self-care and in seeking help when needed.

■ Online Learning Technology

In early uses, online education programs were typically asynchronous (Brown, 2002; Cavanaugh, 2001; Vogel & Klassen, 2001; Yang & Cornelious, 2004). Recent improvements in synchronous technology allow for more interactive discussions, assignments, and exercises. Synchronous technology includes web conferencing, virtual meetings, Blackboard Collaborate, and Adobe Connect (Rockinson-Szapkiw & Walker, 2009).

The students in a hybrid career class were highly satisfied with Elluminate, an Internet class platform that offers chat room discussion, virtual tour of websites, chatting, preloaded slide shows, and other synchronous tools (Ting & Gonzalez, 2013).

Online Discussions

From the research we reviewed, we have gleaned some tips for instructors to improve their online discussions (Brown, 2002; Cavanaugh, 2001). Those tips include:

- Maintain an informal tone built by online discussion.
- Relate online discussion to issues raised in class.
- Structure discussion topics, staying focused around a problem being resolved.
- Define roles for various discussants, such as *original proposer*, *idea extender*, *constructive critic*, *responder to critic*, or *consolidator*.
- Provide incentive for active participation in discussion by providing extra points or enhancing grades for those students.
- Request backup documentation for the points students have raised.
- Keep the discussion board an open and free speech platform.

■ Teaching Clinical Skills and Supervision

One study of skills acquisition in counselor education examined students enrolled in an on-campus and an online introductory counseling skills course (Murdock, Williams, Becker, Bruce, & Young, 2012). The findings show no significant difference between students' basic counseling skill acquisition in either course format.

The counseling skills suggested for online teaching strategies include questioning and probing, reflecting client's feeling, and closing a session. They also make recommendations for helping students to establish and maintain therapeutic relationships online. These recommendations include training counseling students to convey affect with words and symbols, using emoticons, asking the client for clarification, becoming familiar with common and popular and online abbreviations, and keeping a running transcript of the session (Trepal, Haberstroh, Duffey, & Evans, 2007).

U.S. Department of Education Research Methodology

The study was conducted using a rigorous scientific method. The study sample consists of a meta-analysis of 50 study effects, 43 of which were drawn from research with older learners (undergraduate/graduate or adult learners from training programs), and seven of which were with K–12 students. First, more than 50 relevant studies were identified, published from 1996 through 2008; a search result was done by using a common set of keywords. Second, additional searches were done by reviewing articles cited in other meta-analyses and narrative syntheses of research on distance learning (Bernard et al., 2004; Cavanaugh, 2001; Childs, 2001; Sitzmann et al., 2006; Tallent-Runnels et al., 2006). Third, manual searches were conducted to review abstracts for articles published between 2005 and 2008 in the following key journals: *American Journal of Distance Education, Journal of Distance Education* (Canada), *Distance Education* (Australia), *International Review of Research in Distance and Open Education*, and *Journal of Asynchronous Learning Networks*. In addition, the *Journal of Technology and Teacher Education*, and *Career and Technical Education Research* were searched manually. Fourth, the authors explored the Google Scholar search engine with a series of keywords related to online learning. Finally, article abstracts retrieved through these additional search activities were examined to remove duplicates of articles identified earlier.

> *"Research is formalized curiosity. It is poking and prying with a purpose."—Zora Neale Hurston*

References

Bernard, R. M., Abrami, P. C., Lou, Y., Borokhovski, E., Wade, A., Wozney, L., . . . Huang, B. (2004). How does distance education compare with classroom instruction? A meta-analysis of the empirical literature. *Review of Educational Research, 74*(3), 379–439. doi.org/10.3102/00346543074003379

Brown, D. G. (2002). The role you play in online discussion. *Syllabus, 16*(5), 9. Retrieved from https://campustechnology.com/Articles/2002/11/The-Role -you-Play-in-Online-Discussions.aspx

Cavanaugh, C. S. (2001). The effectiveness of interactive distance education technologies in K–12 learning: A meta-analysis. *International Journal of Educational Telecommunications, 7*(1), 73–78. Norfolk, VA: Association for the Advancement of Computing in Education. Retrieved from https:// www.learntechlib.org/p/8461

Childs, J. M. (2001). *Digital skill training research: Preliminary guidelines for distributed learning* (Final report). Albuquerque, NM: TRW.

Clingerman, T. L., & Bernard, J. M. (2004). An investigation of the use of e-mail as a supplemental modality for clinical supervision. *Counselor Education and Supervision, 43*, 82–95. doi:10.1002/j.1556-6978.2004.tb01862.x

Collins, S., & Jerry, P. (2005). The Campus Alberta Applied Psychology Counselling Initiative: Web-based delivery of a graduate professional training program. *Journal of Technology in Human Services, 23*(1&2), 99–119. doi:10.1300/J017v23n01_07

Council for Accreditation of Counseling and Related Educational Programs. (2008). *CACREP 2009 Standards, Section II F*. Retrieved from http://www .cacrep.org/wp-content/uploads/2017/07/2009-Standards.pdf

Ekong, J. I. (2006). What factors facilitate online counselor training? Experiences of Campus Alberta graduate students. *Journal of Distance Education, 21*, 1–14. Retrieved from http://www.ijede.ca/index.php/jde/article/ viewFile/69/50

Krieger, K., & Stockton, R. (2004). Technology and group leadership training: Teaching group counseling in an online environment. *Journal for Specialists in Group Work, 29*, 343–359. doi:10.1080/01933920490516044

Lyke, J., & Frank, M. (2012). Comparison of student learning outcomes in online and traditional classroom environments in a psychology course. *Journal of Instructional Psychology, 39*, 245–250. Retrieved from http://proxying.lib.ncsu.edu/index.php?url=http://search.proquest.com.prox.lib.ncsu.edu/docview/1490691647?accountid=12725

Means, B., Toyama, Y., Murphy, R., Bakia, M., & Jones, K. (2010). *Evaluation of evidence-based practices in online learning: A meta-analysis and review of online learning studies.* Washington, DC: U.S. Department of Education. Retrieved from ERIC database. ERIC Document ED505824.

Merryman, W., Martin, M., & Martin, D. (2015). Relationship between psychological well-being and perceived wellness in online graduate counselor education students. *Journal of Counselor Preparation and Supervision, 7*(1), 3. doi.org/10.7729/71.1073

Moore, M. G. (1994). Administrative barriers to adoption of distance education. *American Journal of Distance Education, 8*(3), 1–4. doi:10.1080/08923649409526862

Murdock, J., Williams, A., Becker, K., Bruce, A. B., & Young, S. (2012). Online versus on-campus: A comparison study of counseling skills courses. *Journal of Human Resources and Adult Learning, 8*(1), 105–118. Retrieved from http://www.hraljournal.com/Page/12%20Jennifer%20Murdock.pdf

Palmer, A., & McBride, D. L. (2012). *Assessing student and faculty satisfaction in a Master of Counselling Distance Education Paradigm* (Master's thesis, Faculty of Education, School of Graduate Studies, University of Lethbridge, Alberta, Canada). Retrieved from ERIC database. Eric Document ED533905.

Rockinson-Szapkiw, A. J., & Walker, V. L. (2009). Web 2.0 technologies: Facilitating interaction in an online human services counseling skills course. *Journal of Technology in Human Services, 27*(3), 175–193. doi:10.1080/15228830903093031

Sitzmann, T., Kraiger, K., Stewart, D., & Wisher, R. (2006). The comparative effectiveness of web-based and classroom instruction: A meta-analysis. *Personnel Psychology, 59*, 623–664. doi:10.1111/j.1744-6570.2006.00049.x

Smith, R. L., Flamez, B., Vela, J. C., Schomaker, S. A., Fernandez, M. A., & Armstrong, S. N. (2015). An exploratory investigation of levels of learning and learning efficiency between online and face-to-face instruction. *Counseling Outcome Research and Evaluation, 6*, 47–57. doi:10.1177/2150137815572148

Tallent-Runnels, M., Thomas, J., Lan, W., Cooper, S., Ahern, T., Shaw, S., & Liu, X. (2006). Teaching Courses Online: A Review of the Research. Review Of Educational Research, 76(1), 93–135. doi:10.3102/00346543076001093

Ting, S. R. (2016). *Evaluation of an online counseling program.* Paper presented at the Eleventh International Conference on Teaching, Education, and Learning, London, UK.

Ting, S. R., & Gonzalez, L. (2013). Quality of interactions in face-to-face and hybrid career development courses: An exploration of students' perceptions. *Journal of Online Learning and Teaching, 9,* 316–327. Retrieved from http://jolt.merlot.org/vol9no3/ting_0913.htm

Trepal, H., Haberstroh, S., Duffey, T., & Evans, M. (2007). Considerations and strategies for teaching online counseling skills: Establishing relationships in cyberspace. *Counselor Education and Supervision, 46,* 226–279. doi:10.1002/j.1556-6978.2007.tb00031.x

Vogel, D., & Klassen, J. (2001). Technology-supported learning: Status, issues and trends. *Journal of Computer Assisted Learning, 17,* 104–114. doi:10.1111/j.1365-2729.2001.00163.x

Wisher, R. A., & Olson, T. M. (2003). *The effectiveness of web-based training* (Research Report No. 1802). Alexandria, VA: U.S. Army Research Institute.

Yang, Y., & Cornelious, L. F. (2004, October). *Ensuring quality in online education instructions: What instructors should know?* Paper presented at the annual meeting of the Association for Educational Communications and Technology, Chicago, IL. Retrieved from ERIC database. ERIC Document ED484990.

Zhao, Y., Lei, J., Yan, B., Lai, C., & Tan, H. S. (2005). What makes the difference? A practical analysis of research on the effectiveness of distance education. *Teachers College Record, 107*(8), 1836–1884. doi:10.1111/j.1467-9620.2005.00544.x

Roadmap to Online Instruction in the Helping Professions: Practical Steps and Considerations for Success

In this chapter, we focus on practical steps and thoughtful considerations to help you design a successful online course and curriculum. This chapter addresses both instructors and administrators, providing tips and checklists to think through before, during, and after the semester.

VIGNETTE

At the end of the fall semester, the department head asked me to teach a "Cross-Cultural Counseling" course using both the synchronous and asynchronous environments. I have taught the course for several years on campus but never taught an online course before. Reluctantly, I said yes.

I felt overwhelmed with all the moving parts. My mind was overloaded with the technological jargon, the technology itself, questions about how to get started, what resources were available at my university, and how to go about structuring a course for good student involvement and outcomes.

This seemed like a huge project to me, and I knew better than to try to figure it out on my own or wing it, so I began by researching best practices for course design and talking to colleagues who had taught online before. At the time, not many university instructors had ventured into the online teaching world within the helping professions. Some of the best advice I received was from the instructional technologists at my university; they suggested that I "dip my toe" in the water when creating a course rather than attempting a large-scale project right off the bat, as this can be a steep learning curve. I didn't find that the online platforms were too difficult or cumbersome to learn, but when I needed help, the technologists walked me through it step by step.

I made some mistakes along the way, but I discovered that the students and the technology were more forgiving than I expected. My biggest error was not scheduling enough time before the semester began to interpret my on-campus pedagogy into online pedagogy. I also learned that course consistency and success (as well as my sanity) hinge on having in place— before the semester begins—the course design and a plan for intentional relationship building with the students.

OVERARCHING QUESTIONS

1. What do I need to learn about teaching online in an asynchronous and synchronous space?
2. What tasks do I need to complete to create the course in an online environment?
3. In developing the course, course objectives, and lesson plans, what needs to happen before, during, and after the course to create a productive, interactive, and positive learning experience for the students?
4. How might your use of time be spent differently in an on-campus class versus an online course? For example, consider how long it takes for you to prepare a lesson plan for an on-campus class and how this might differ from preparing an online course.
5. What considerations do administrators give to the delivery of online courses and programs?

■ So You Want to Be an Online Instructor . . .

The Importance of Time

Time is one part of life that we all wish we had more of, but we can't seem to create or free up more. Knowing this, instructors and administrators need to recognize and remember that time may look different in the online environment compared to the on-campus classroom setting; it certainly is used differently.

For instructors, the time needed for preparation and delivery of the content is vastly different than the time needed for on-campus courses. Instructors need to plan ahead and prepare for courses strategically and systematically. "Flying by the seat of your pants" in the online environment is not recommended. It will lead to a stressful semester for everyone.

Everything takes more time to prepare and deliver online than in person. For example, preparing a lesson plan means not simply typing out the lesson;

rather, it requires that you take the time to structure, upload, and organize the content in the learning management system (LMS). Additionally, intentionally adding engagement opportunities for students to connect throughout the asynchronous and synchronous session is an important element to build into your planning and time schedule.

WORD TO THE WISE: No one wants to work 24/7 in their position, and we do not get paid to do so. It is helpful to set apart time for work in your schedule. Thereafter, sharing your preferred schedule and expectations with your students about communication is also vital to the success of your course. Be sure to incorporate self-care activities into your routine. Modeling self-care strategies and your availability, as well as setting healthy limitations and boundaries, is part of demonstrating effective practices within the helping professions. For example, as you set expectations about your availability, you can share with students that they would not anticipate being on call with their clients 24/7, which could lead to burnout and possibly leaving the position or profession. We all need self-care . . . instructors included!

Planning Content

As you plan the course, consider what content is best suited for asynchronous versus synchronous sessions. How can you best use the time based on the learning objectives, goals, and time allotted? Some ideas or examples can be read or self-taught, whereas others have to be shared verbally, and other concepts must be modeled in our own actions through our engagement with our students. Consider what technology you have that will most effectively support the information you are trying to impart.

Learning theory should not be overlooked when developing and delivering online instruction. As you may know, the zone of proximal development is a concept coined by Lev Vygotsky. In online classes or programs, it is important to provide instruction as well as assignments that are developmentally appropriate or within students' zone of proximal development. Understanding students' level of competency in technology use as well as general growth and development in the program is critical. Considering the zone of proximal development, instructors can best design assignments that meet students "where they are." For example, the required use of a certain technology can impede some students' ability to demonstrate competency regarding a given standard or student learning outcome. Alternatively, a range or variety of technologies can be offered to complete the assignment. Recognizing the collective zone of proximal development (e.g., first semester of program) of students can promote growth and development while allowing students the opportunity to focus on the curriculum rather than the medium through which it is delivered or digested.

Instructors should also consider social cognitive theory (SCT) when working with students. SCT highlights the roles of observation and modeling in an individual's education. The personal and professional attitudes and behaviors conveyed through instruction and related interaction often are observed by students and in some cases internalized as they matriculate through coursework and into the field. Instructors must remain cognizant of the dispositions they model and the ways in which those dispositions affect instruction. Organization, time management, and attention to detail, among others, are instructor variables that influence students' perceived experiences of a course.

Online tools and resources such as discussion threads or audio and video tools are useful for modeling professional attitudes and behaviors. It is important that posts, in discussion threads especially, be written with care and concern so as not to be misinterpreted or taken out of context.

Instructors can incorporate videos to offer guidance and instruction on the use of technology or concepts presented in course textbooks and lectures. Many resources are readily available via the Internet. Other resources can be developed by instructors as needed.

Finally, the work of Benjamin Bloom in the mid-1950s has had a lasting impact on education. Bloom's taxonomy was designed to promote higher order thinking skills in the classroom. The taxonomy has evolved since 1956, but it still remains relevant in today's classrooms. Though most often used in the K–12 setting, the taxonomy also is applicable in higher education and specifically online learning. Using the taxonomy in the development of discussion prompts and assignments can ensure that students are thinking about the course content critically and in a number of ways. Table 6.1 offers a glimpse into the ways in which questions and prompts can be developed based on the taxonomy.

With learning theory in mind, the following data, tips, activities, checklists, and considerations are provided to help both new online instructors and new online program administrators think through the process of online education throughout the semester—before classes begin, during the flow of the semester, and after the semester has concluded.

Table 6.1 Level of questions

Level of Question	Example of Question
Create	Develop strategies or a model counselors can use to ensure that they demonstrate empathy.
Evaluate	Observe a mock counseling session and appraise the degree of empathy demonstrated by the counselor.
Analyze	Differentiate between the client relationships and outcomes of an empathetic vs. nonempathetic counselor.
Apply	Demonstrate empathy in a mock counseling session.
Understand	Describe the characteristics of an empathetic counselor.
Remember	Define empathy.

It is important for administrators to think of the "big picture" when considering online course or program delivery. Program directors and department chairs are often responsible for the administration of online courses and programs, including the development, implementation, and maintenance of those courses/programs. For administrators, the development of courses or programs begins well before the start of the semester. Implementation and maintenance of online courses and programs extend well beyond the conclusion of the semester.

FOR ADMINISTRATORS

Are you considering establishing an online program? Or maybe you are interested in converting campus-based courses into an online or hybrid format. If so, here are a few considerations:

- What is the current and future interest in online learning at your institution?
- Who are the stakeholders and interested constituents both in the student body and the administration?
- Does your institution have the technological capacity and support for an online program?
- What is the process for establishing new programs or converting course formats at your university?
- What levels of approval are needed for the initiative?
- Is there campus-wide support for the initiative?
- How will the new online program be marketed?
- Is there compensation (e.g., stipend or release time) to offset the time required to develop the program?
- Who is your target audience?
    - Current students
    - Alumni
    - Community practitioners
    - Other helping professionals
- In what time zones will your students reside?
- Location: USA or international?
- What is the fee or credit hour per class required for the program?
- How much is tuition?
- Will the course meet the current guidelines of the State Board (where the student is located)?
- Who will be responsible for the administration of the course or program?

Before the Semester

Perhaps online course offerings or an online program are already established at your university. If so, congratulations! Even so, there still are many logistical and instructional concerns that must be addressed prior to the start of the semester. Though not an exhaustive list, here are a few items administrators should consider:

- Who will teach the online course?
- Has the course already been developed for an online environment?
- Does the faculty member have sufficient expertise in content and online course delivery?
- Is there sufficient enrollment or demand for the course?
- Is the course offered during a time that is conducive to proper program matriculation?
- Does the offering align or fit into the course rotation model for the program?
- Does the instructor have sufficient access to the course shell and syllabi?
- Are there opportunities to strengthen the course based on student/instructor feedback from the last semester?
- What level of support does the instructor require? A peer-mentor? Training?

WORD TO THE WISE: When setting dates and times for synchronous courses, consider the time zone and where the students are located, especially if the course/program is open to international students. One of the authors had a student in Italy who had to join the course synchronous sessions from 11 p.m. to midnight in her time zone in order to attend the interactive sessions.

Many tasks associated with these items should be completed well before the start of the semester, in many cases during the previous semester. What other tasks can you think of that are important for administrators to consider?

_____

_____

_____

During the Semester

Similar to the beginning of a semester, tasks are plentiful during the semester. Although instructors are largely responsible for the delivery of instruction, it is important for administrators to support their efforts. Here are a few suggestions:

- Request and review course syllabi to ensure that they are compliant with university policies and meet accreditation guidelines (if applicable).
- Ensure that instructors are aware of census/roster verification dates, add/drop, withdrawal, and academic advising dates and deadlines. Encourage instructors to remind students of this information.

- Check in regularly with instructors to field any questions or concerns they may have.
- Conduct announced pop-ins during class meetings (asynchronous and synchronous).
- Ensure that instructor and course evaluations are disseminated to students.
- Ensure that course and program data are collected for program assessment.
- Offer and disseminate instructional information or professional development opportunities and encourage instructor attendance.
- Begin to prepare for the next semester (e.g., course offerings, textbooks, instructors).

Identify two more "mid-semester" responsibilities of administrators:

_____

_____

At the Conclusion of the Semester

As the semester comes to a close, administrators remain occupied with many and varied tasks. It is important to end the semester as fluidly as it began. Administrators are encouraged to consider the following items when determining how to wrap up a semester:

- Disseminate course/instructor evaluations to appropriate instructors.
- Read students' evaluations/reviews of instructors/courses.
- Provide feedback to instructors and develop plan/goals for undertaking whatever is necessary for improvement.
- Continue to establish a comfort level with sharing feedback and the overall evaluation process.
- Write and disseminate instructor evaluations.
- Identify, define, or create a process for closing out the course.
- What level of access do students have to the course following the semester termination of the course?
- Should we shut down the course? If you continue to provide access, what is the time limit?
- Who will have access to the course after it is taught? Is it a course shell that is shared among instructors or teaching assistants (TAs)?
- Deal with confidentiality issues in relation to content. A related consideration is to think about TAs who may have access to the course content and also have future interactions with students in the class on a peer or supervisory level as well.
- Who "owns" and has rights to the course after it has been created?

What other considerations are there for administrators at the end of the semester?

_____

_____

FOR INSTRUCTORS

There is a lot for instructors to do before the semester begins, but there is no need to feel overwhelmed. Take a deep breath and dive right in! Here is a checklist of things to consider and do to get your course and yourself ready on time. Keep the KISS acronym and principle in mind: Keep it simple, stupid (Interaction Design Foundation, n.d.). This acronym can be a reminder when you begin to feel overwhelmed and overthink the course design.

One Month Out (or Less)

The first step is to get answers to who, what, when, and where.

- Where and how will you offer the course? All online? Or hybrid? Or blended?
- Has the course been offered online before?
- What is the length of the course?
- Will you co-teach or have a teaching assistant?
- How many students?
- When will you order your textbooks through your university bookstore? Are there deadlines to consider?
- Is there an online option for students to purchase books and have them delivered directly to homes or offices? If so, how will you communicate this to students?

Course Design

What technological support is available at your institution? Check with your institution to see if it offers an online course about how to teach online. Also check if other resources are offered for faculty.

Identify the LMS and other technology you will use and become familiar with the software. Attend workshops and training sessions through the distance education office or office of technology at your university. Some trainings will be offered on campus and others online through prerecorded on-campus workshops.

Determine the space where you will teach your courses online. For example, will you teach online in your office on campus, at home, or where? Set up your space in a way that exudes calm, comfort, and peace to engage freely with your students. Be sure the space is quiet, confidential, and free from distractions.

Download or purchase the technology and tools that your university uses to your computer.

Test your log-in to the online accounts you will be using for your course (i.e., all technology you plan to use, including your LMS).

If the course is new, discuss with your department and administration whether or not you will be provided with an instructional designer to assist you with the design of your course. In some cases, you can apply for grants to provide funding to hire instructional designers to help you build and design it.

If the course has been taught online before, contact the distance education office to locate your course shell or identify how to copy a preexisting course to the new semester within the LMS.

Have you taught this course in an on-campus format? If so, consider ways to adapt the content for online delivery. Consider how you will update and adapt lectures, presentations, activities, and other teaching methods used in traditional teaching environments. Do not assume that face-to-face teaching will translate seamlessly to the online classroom. For example, online lectures should be no more than 10 minutes long; consider your audience and their attention span.

Find out from the program if there is a preexisting syllabus or if one must be created. Some universities offer online syllabus templates for instructors to build their syllabus using a standardized online format.

Quality Matters (www.qualitymatters.org) is a comprehensive website to aid online instructors in designing successful, student-centered courses. It is a subscription service that relies on data from both peer review and professional design review of submitted courses. It is a great resource if you are just starting out.

Your best resource is the technology and/or distance education office at your university or within your department.

Course Development Roadmap

As you begin to develop your online course, keep in mind the syllabus and course objectives, because, within the helping professions, many programs must adhere to and comply with the requirements and standards of accreditation bodies to remain accredited. Aligning your learning objectives and outcomes with the applicable accreditation standards (e.g., CACREP and CSWE) is imperative.

As you plan for the course, connect with your institution or department to learn if the course is intended to be offered as an all-online course, hybrid, or blended course offering. Each program and institution may have its own standards and structure. As the instructor, in some cases, there will be some latitude to make this decision, but usually the delivery method will be set for you. If you have a preference as to the delivery method, indicate your preferred interests early on in the process in order for the scheduling office to note in the registration/course catalog how the course will be offered. This becomes particularly important when offering courses as hybrids (i.e., online and on-campus).

Additionally, synchronous sessions should to be indicated in the registration process so that students know and understand the requirements and specific dates for on-campus meetings prior to registering for the course. The rationale for sharing the dates and times of on-campus meetings is to give students the ability to prepare and plan ahead for required meetings. Adult students often have packed evenings and weekends and appreciate knowing the expectations of on-campus or synchronous required meetings when they register. Share this information early and reiterate the expectations at the beginning of the semester.

As you delve into course design, consider the learning objectives for your course.

- What do you want your students to gain from the experience?
- What are the anticipated learning outcomes?
- How will your students learn the material? (e.g., mini-lectures, engaging activities, role plays, journal reflections, discussions, case studies, presentations, group work, textbook, other outside resources, current events).
- How will the students demonstrate understanding? Through an assessment, evaluation, role play, practice, demonstration, reflective activity, journal, and so forth?
- How will you evaluate the students online? Will you need to use a proctor, video recordings, written submissions, online quizzes, and so forth? Does your university have a testing center that offers a proctor and testing location if needed?

When creating "lesson plans," it can be helpful to create a spreadsheet with four simple columns to organize each week's plan visually:

1. Title of the content, including course objectives and standards
2. Course details
3. Instructional materials: activities and task related to the topic
4. Activities/Engagement/Assessment/Evaluation: outcomes/deliverables (e.g., quiz, paper, etc.)

This serves as an outline or roadmap for the course for the number of weeks in the semester.

Your spreadsheet might look like Table 6.2. Review Chapter 12 for specific details about instructional design and for more information about structuring your course to meet your needs and standards.

Table 6.2 Learning Objectives

Week 1: Title, Objectives, and Standards	Course Details	Instructional Materials (text, video, etc.)	Activities Engagement/ Assessment/ Evaluation

Build

Great courses are intentionally built! The building process includes locating and "chunking" content according to the syllabus and uploading it all into weekly modules that are released or "opened" to the students sequentially. The use of scaffolding is a common best practice within teaching, whereby topics are broken into parts and those parts build upon one another.

First, create an outline for your course and begin building the content, including information from the textbook, activities, assignments, engaging polls and quizzes, tests, assessments, videos, lectures, recordings, rubrics, discussion board questions, and so forth. As you identify course content, organize the material based on specified dates in the syllabus.

Create a link to the student honor code to add to the student center in the LMS. The university student honor code serves as a protective measure if and when students violate the honor code. Plagiarism is a good example of a violation.

Build the module depending on the method of delivery for the course. The synchronous session should be used for practice, experimenting, role plays, small and large group discussion, presentations, and other engaging activities. Lectures in this environment should be held to a minimum and a flipped classroom model is recommended.

Asynchronous classes require weekly modules that are engaging and very detailed. (See Chapter 8 for more information on group work, activities, assessment, testing, breakout rooms, and discussion boards.)

Consistency in the look and feel of the format is important for students to easily navigate the online content.

One resource to keep in mind as you create your course is the Open Educational Resources Commons where you can search, share, and review lessons, modules, graphics, and so forth for free (www.oercommons.org).

Copyright laws: As you collect images, pictures, and graphs for your course, be aware of copyright laws, and become familiar with the regulations for online teaching. Visit the copyright office at your institution for more information and also check out information about the Technology, Education and Copyright Harmonization Act (TEACH Act) for more specific details on copyright rules and regulations (www.copyright.gov/title17/92chap1.html).

After the syllabus is complete and assignments are created, venture into the LMS to build your grade book. Some systems allow for automatic grading and grade recording of multiple-choice quizzes. You can use points or percentages depending on your preference and the LMS you are using.

As you begin building the course in Moodle, create a student center as an introductory module that will hold and capture important information for students. Some items may include the syllabus, instructor contact information, instructions and tutorials for the technology that is used in the course, tentative learning schedule including due dates for assignments, contact information for requesting accommodations, expectations for the course, the dates and/or links for synchronous sessions, resources related to the content, a cyber "café" where students can connect and network, and so forth.

Check that all the dates you have entered match the dates in your syllabus. If they do not, you will receive multiple emails from the students regarding the conflicting dates. If you change dates in the LMS, be sure to update the dates on the syllabus, and vice versa.

If you have specific course materials or articles for students to view through the on-campus library, most universities offer a way to link the online library with the LMS. Instructors can request a course reserve for students to view specific course materials related to the content area. Embedding the link to the online library allows students to access the library without having to leave the LMS.

10 Days Before the Semester

Begin crafting your welcome letter. The welcome letter should be sent to students about 1 week before the semester. It includes this type of information:

- The syllabus and textbook information
- A welcome letter to the class (optional; welcome video using YouTube, PowToon, or other video software)
- Information on required technology
- User ID/password information
- Links for your course software (e.g., Moodle, Blackboard Collaborate)
- Tech tutorials
- The contact information for technical support (you may want to ask IT support for their frequently asked questions/FAQs)
- Information for students as to when they will receive grades, the process for submitting the grade to the licensure board, and so forth

See Chapter 8 for more details on the welcome letter.

Script your course. If you are teaching a synchronous class, it will be exceedingly helpful for you if you come prepared with a detailed script that highlights the lesson plan and material to be covered moment by moment along with the procedures. For example, if you decide to use a polling feature, what steps would you need to take to poll students and publish the results? Build in extra time for "moving" students into breakout rooms and back to the main room. Also, extend the time that you think an activity will take by at least 10 minutes.

Consider having a practice session that lets you deliver content in the synchronous space prior to your first "live" session. This will build up your confidence and help you identify any issues or glitches that may arise.

Ideally, you will have a teaching assistant or graduate assistant to work with you during each session to help manage the chat box, student questions, and other logistics. Co-teaching can be very useful when there are so many tasks to complete simultaneously in a "live" online classroom.

Keep accessibility in mind. How accessible is your course for all students? Have you accommodated your students' needs? It is important to remember to use ADA-compliant resources, videos, recordings, and so forth. Check with your institution's Americans with Disabilities Act office to help you think through how you can make your course accessible to all students. Grackle.com offers help and information in making accessible documents. Time permitting, record and/or narrate the syllabus to be uploaded as an additional link to the LMS. Adding closed captioning can also be another option.

One Week Out

Send out the welcome letter. It is important to allow enough time for students to thoroughly read the syllabus, test the LMS, click on the links, and "play" in the space before class begins.

Add the finishing touches to your module: graphics, music, polls, guests, videos, quotes, and so forth.

Log in and test the system. Recheck that all videos and links work. Make sure to check the "student view" so that you know they are seeing what you want them to see.

During the Semester

Day One

Synchronous: Log into the system at least a few hours prior to class beginning to allow time to deal with any issues that may pop up at the last minute. Set up your class and ensure that it is ready before students enter the space. Upload any documents and items that you will be covering during your session. For example, if you plan to use a PowerPoint presentation, upload it a few hours beforehand in case there are any unforeseen issues.

Asynchronous: For a 15-week course, it is ideal for you to have your content for the first few weeks of the course ready to go by this point. Instructors can open the week 1 learning module and the student center for students to view on the first week while building and updating weeks 2 to 15 as the semester goes.

WORD TO THE WISE: The more you can accomplish and build before the semester begins, the easier your life will be.

30 Minutes Before

Get a glass of water, go to the bathroom, set up your desk space and lighting, keep your phone and other devices in silent mode, and put your first day script in front of you. Clear your space, so you are free of distractions.

Go Live!

Arrive in the class space early to make sure that everything is in order.

Add a link to an upbeat song or calming instrumental music to the synchronous space for students to click on and enjoy when they enter the online space.

Welcome students into the class as you see them arrive by sending a welcome note in the chat box.

First-Day Introductions

In courses in the helping professions, it is so important to make an extra effort at getting the students settled in and helping them get to know each other and you. Making introductions on the first day of class breaks down barriers, invites open conversation, and invigorates class morale. The key is to make these initial activities fun and personal without being too private or invasive. The technological design of the course—synchronous or asynchronous—determines how the introductions are made. In Chapter 8, we offer a few examples of first-day introduction activities for both types of environments to help you think through the possibilities of this foundation-building event. An added bonus to these exercises is that it invites the students to explore the tools offered in the online system on the very first day so that questions and technical difficulties can be addressed up front. Much like the beginning of a therapeutic alliance, the first sessions of the online course are intended to get to know each other, build a solid foundation of trust and rapport, and provide a welcoming space to ask questions, learn, and grow.

It is also important to explicitly state on the first day that the course is designed for instruction in supervision in lieu of being an opportunity to receive supervision and/or therapeutic help. This is a good time to review standards and ethics regarding privacy, confidentiality, and maintaining those standards online.

Here are a few more tips for the flow of the semester:

- Maintain the course structure and follow the syllabus.
- Remain visible and available.
- Remember that instructors are "gatekeepers." Faculty within the helping professions have the ethical responsibility to monitor and protect the profession as students in the helping professions matriculate from social work, counseling, psychology, marriage and family therapy (MFT), and other programs and serve the community.
- For synchronous classes, log on early to field questions before class and stay after for follow-up questions.
- If possible, record the sessions and share with students how to access the recordings.
- Include Q&A sessions to build rapport with your students.
- Remember to assess the progress of the course with your students sometime during the course of the semester, preferably checking in with students several times throughout the semester.

After

After the semester ends, there are a few tasks left to do:

- Seek feedback in formal and informal ways from students, peers, and administrators.
- Grade all assignments, discussion boards, presentations, and so forth. Return assignments to students with feedback, and add grades to your LMS.
- Submit final grades to students and the institution according to predetermined expectations.
- Consider the length of time to keep the course open after it ends for students to collect each other's contact information and preserve course data.
- Set the stage for ongoing professional development.
- Discuss future resources with the students and ideas for staying connected after the course: websites, trainings, email exchanges, and so forth.

Post-Semester Administrative Tasks

- Consider who "owns" the rights to the content and course design.
- How long do you and your students have access to the content in the LMS? (e.g., 3 months, 6 months, forever)
- Do you have the ability to copy content to recycle it for a future course to save yourself some time and energy? How do you go about doing so?
- Reflect upon whether or not to create and update the course in a "play space" so that you can make adaptations and changes to enhance the course for the next time it is offered.

Post-Semester Review

Take 20 minutes to reflect for yourself on the design of the course, how the class went, how the students felt about the course, and how you felt about the course. This intentional reflection is for your own growth and course improvement.

- Review your student evaluations and feedback. Consider feasible strategies for areas you would like to improve upon in the future.
- Talk to other instructors about ways they teach their courses and ask if you could view or sit in on one of their courses during the downtime between semesters.
- Celebrate! You did it!!! Go to dinner, and enjoy some self-care!

REFLECTIVE QUESTIONS

These reflective questions will help you start your journey toward online instructing. By spending just a few minutes reflecting on your own skills, contacts, and resources, and writing your thoughts and brainstorms, you will create a handy guide for yourself.

1. What strengths do you bring to the helping profession that can be translated into online teaching modalities?

Strength 1:

_____

Strength 2:

_____

Perhaps you are an expert in your content area, a charismatic facilitator, your personal pedagogical style has great outcomes, or you develop solid relationships with your students. Can you think of characteristics or traits that are related to you?

2. What characteristics do you possess that will be beneficial as an online instructor?

Characteristic 1:

_____

Characteristic 2:

_____

Are you knowledgeable in your field, an expert in the content area? Do you have a strong ability to identify resources within the field or respond to students in a timely manner? What other characteristics might you possess?

3. What resources do you have at your university to support your online teaching and what continuous education/training in online instruction does your institution offer?

Resource 1:

_____

Resource 2:

_____

Consider if these resources are available to you: library staff, office of faculty development, technology department or organization of information technology, other faculty who have taught online (even if they are outside of your discipline), and so forth.

4. List two colleagues in the helping professions or another field that you could contact for support, encouragement, advice, and content knowledge about online instruction.

Contact 1: (name/email)

_____

Contact 2: (name/email)

_____

Think about the professionals and colleagues within your department and immediate scope. It is good to also consider mentors, former faculty, and new and incoming faculty who have expertise and interest in using technology. Also consider prior teachers, role models, colleagues within private practice or within the university setting, and so forth. Former students can also be a source of input and highlight specific information about ways to improve your teaching practice and incorporate technology and share with you what you are doing well.

WORD TO THE WISE: Create a document for each course, and make a list of questions for review after the semester. For example, create a Google Doc or spreadsheet. Take 10 minutes to review your syllabus and make notes on any of the changes and/or adaptations you want to make to the syllabus, structure, assignments, in-class assignments, content timing, content, organization of material for the course (layout), and any other changes. If you are strapped for time, create a video and record yourself using your phone or other device, and talk through the semester or syllabus while highlighting any changes you would like to make the next time you teach the course. Review the recording as you plan for teaching the course in the future.

■ Takeaways

1. Know your advocates, support systems, resources, and cheerleaders.

2. Manage your time wisely and prepare for the unexpected. Build in extra time for potential challenges or mishaps. Identify the best time management system for you: are you a pen-and-paper planner, or someone who appreciates an app, software, or electronic planner? The Together Group (www.thetogethergroup.com) is an online resource for teachers that includes helpful tips, videos, examples, and additional publications. Other tools that we find helpful are Evernote, Google calendars, Doodle, and Wunderlist.

3. Think about your own self-care during this process: it can be challenging, overwhelming, and stressful to consider teaching and designing a course, especially if you have never done it before. Online meditation and relaxation apps such as Headspace; Stop, Think, and Breathe; and Calm may help you stay relaxed and present. How do you best de-stress and unwind during stressful times in your life?

HELPFUL TIP: Instructors should not assume that because they have taught a seated course on campus that the experience seamlessly moves to an online course. It requires a great deal of intentional planning and thought to move content and instruction online.

"Every goal has its own roadmap to success."—Lily Tomlin

Resources

Borders, L. D., & Brown, L. L. (2005). *The new handbook of counseling supervision.* Mahwah, NJ: Lawrence Erlbaum.

Ko, S., & Rossen, S. (2004). *Teaching online: A practical guide.* Boston, MA: Houghton Mifflin.

YouTube videos:
Good and bad demos of clinical supervision (employment setting): www.youtube.com/watch?v=S9iDB_9njMw&feature=related

Latino-centered supervision role-play from American Counseling Association 2012 Conference and Exposition, March 21–25, San Franciso, CA. Retrieved From www.youtube.com/watch?v=7yxPkkSnmDk&feature=related

The reluctant supervisee: Texas supervision workshop: www.youtube.com/watch?v=wfWvWDymehY&feature=related

Professionalism in clinical supervision: www.youtube.com/watch?v=RQQLUobn2xE&feature=related

Second life online supervision: www.youtube.com/watch?v=G__KJsoPnqA&feature=related

Reference

Interaction Design Foundation. (n.d.). *KISS (keep it simple, stupid): A design principle.* Retrieved from https://www.interaction-design.org/literature/article/kiss-keep-it-simple-stupid-a-design-principle

Student-Focused Classroom: Resources for Helping Your Students to Be Successful Online Learners

VIGNETTE

On my syllabi, I include a "tentative learning agenda" to highlight the specific chapters, tests, assignments, etc., required along with the due dates for each listing. It is a table embedded at the end of the syllabus and uploaded as a separate document in the learning management system (LMS) to give students a quick snapshot of the major assignments and due dates. Including this information in a table format enhances ease of viewing and allows students to "check off" tasks as they move through the semester. The tentative learning agenda provides a roadmap for the course and keeps everyone on the same page.

As changes occur, they can be posted in the LMS in the student center or specific location designated by the instructor. To be successful online learners, I encourage my students to consistently check back with the tentative learning agenda on the syllabus.

OVERARCHING QUESTIONS

1. What are several concrete steps your students can take to become successful online learners?
2. What resources and/or other items do your students need to purchase or consider before the semester/course begins (e.g., laptop, headphones, microphone, calendar)?
3. What are your students' preferred learning styles?

Like it or not, in our current academic culture, student reviews can make or break an instructor's career. It may not matter that the student did poorly in the class because of a lack of student initiative, low tech savviness, or a general lack of preparedness for online learning—all things that are out of the instructor's natural purview and certainly beyond the instructor's control. So, it behooves you as an instructor to offer resources and assistance that will help your students be effective *learners*. We present this chapter to help you recognize practical student needs and simple methods to address those needs.

Think back to your own learning experiences as a student. What classes did you learn the most from in the face-to-face environment? In which format did you learn best (e.g., instructional, lectures, engaging, hands-on activities)? How might your students' ability to receive information look different in an online environment? For example, consider how preparation and management might look different for classes offered completely online asynchronously, hybrid, and/or all online with various components offered live (i.e., synchronously).

As a student engages in an online course, there are expectations about the time and amount of preparation required for success. In 3-hour, graduate-level asynchronous courses, students can anticipate spending 5 to 10 hours per week online. For a hybrid course, students should expect to spend some time in-person/face-to-face with the instructor and other students to practice skills and discuss the material covered in the LMS. This could mean meeting once a week for 1 to 3 hours, meeting every other week, meeting once a month, or meeting for a live half-a-day or full-day weekend session once a semester in addition to weekly course content.

It is important for students to identify the type of format in which the online course is offered when preparing for the semester. It is also important for your students to consider their learning style before registering and decide whether or not to take the course or engage in an online program at all. Instructors can help prospective students navigate these types of complicated decisions. This chapter is intended to support you, the instructor, as you provide information about the online learning environment to your prospective and current students.

■ Reflective Checklist for Your Students

The checklist can be shared with students to gain a quick snapshot of the type of online learners they may be. We can learn a lot from these types of checklists. Instructors can post the information online for students to respond to in a private discussion forum, or upload it as an assignment.

☐   In the past, how did you prefer to receive information from your instructors/ teachers?

_____

_____

☐   What is your learning style?

_____

_____

☐   Do you prefer to learn using auditory, kinesthetic, visual, or other media?

_____

_____

☐   Reflection on these experiences: what worked for you and what didn't?

_____

_____

☐   What other questions might you ask your students to learn more about their preferred learning style, level of content expertise, comfort with technology, and so forth?

_____

_____

■ Before the Semester: Preparing Students

You can help your students prepare for your course, the technology, and the ethics specific to the helping professions before classes begin. I like to send my students a checklist to prioritize tasks that must be accomplished before the first day of class.

Student Checklist

☐   Become familiar with the format of the class.

☐   Connect with the instructor via email or through another method so that we can get to know each other. It is also an opportunity to clarify any gaps in understanding about the format, syllabus, content, delivery of the material, required textbooks and additional or optional readings, how and when grades are given, and so forth.

☐   Ask the instructor about and purchase the appropriate versions and type of technology (e.g., headset, computer, video equipment) to be a successful learner.

☐   Attend an orientation if offered by the institution, program, or instructor.

☐   It is advantageous to start early in preparing for the class and/or program.

Many programs offer an orientation to the course, program, and technology. Instructors can share with students about the support structure that may already be in place at the university. Part of reducing anxiety for students is limiting or eliminating the "unknowns" in the equation of learning online before the semester begins.

■ During the Semester

Time Management

Planning ahead and placing all due dates and class meeting times on your calendar prior to the beginning of the semester will be a lifesaver for you during the semester. Consider how you manage your time most effectively. Are you one to review your LMS every day and schedule a designated time on your calendar to review and respond to students online? What time of day are you most available and best suited to respond to emails and student comments? Keep your working style and energy levels in mind when you consider managing your time during the semester. Plot out times for advising, required faculty meetings, and other mandatory meetings first, then build your calendar for online instruction around these requirements. Throughout the semester, assess how things are going. Are you finding yourself tired or overwhelmed? Build in time for self-care and a "plan B" in the event the initial plan is derailed by that unexpected meeting or student issue that arises.

WORD TO THE WISE: Share these time management tips with your students to help them juggle their classes, work, family time, and other responsibilities.

Understanding Assessments and Grading

Instructors will determine how they will measure learning outcomes depending on the course content. Some assessment types may include online quizzes, participation grades, short papers, research papers, discussion forum posts, multiple-choice exams, take-home exams (i.e., open book), reflective papers, journals, and other assignments required for the course. One big tip is to become extremely familiar with your syllabus and know where it is located in the LMS. Share with your students that, when in doubt, refer back to the details and expectations provided by the instructor.

Midterm Self-Assessment for the Student

At some point in the first half of the semester, taking time to reflect on what is or is not working for students can be beneficial for outcomes in the course. A few reflection questions to pose to students may include the following:

- How much time am I spending each week on the course? Is the amount of time conducive to completing all assignments and responsibilities?

- How is my relationship with my instructor? Do we have an open dialogue of communication? Why or why not? Am I satisfied with the level of communication? If not, what are concrete steps I can take to improve it?

- Review current technology use for the course: What is working? What adaptations should or could be made? Do I need to purchase or explore the university options for any additional resources to be more effective as a learner?

- How am I feeling about the content of the course?

- What is the relationship like with my colleagues/other students in the program? Are there ways to connect and communicate even more effectively to enhance our professional relationship(s)?

Instructor's Midterm or Periodic Assessment

Share with your students that you may periodically solicit feedback on what is working well and what adaptations can be made to enhance student experience. This request gives students the space to provide anonymous feedback, so be sure to tell them that their input will not influence their grade.

One approach the instructor could take is to ask the students to describe each task they are working on in the course by using red, yellow, or green to indicate the pace and interest in proceeding with various content, concepts, and activities.

Red: things we should "stop" doing in our class.

Yellow: do we slow down the pace or adapt the class process?

Green: this color indicates what you enjoy about the course and continue to practice and proceed as planned in the online environment.

Asking students for feedback through this simple exercise can glean valuable information to help you plan your next steps in this course and in future courses.

In processing feedback, instructors should not identify specific student information, but rather synthesize the comments and use it to make changes in the course. It may be possible for some changes to take place immediately, while other changes may not be feasible given the amount of time remaining in the semester. Typically, there is another opportunity to provide more formal feedback at the end of the course. The evaluation is often sent through a survey disseminated by the department or university to gain feedback from students about the course in order to evaluate the instructor's performance.

▪ After the Semester

It's Not Over Until It's Over

At the end of the semester, there are a few final tasks for students to consider before they close out the semester or experience. Here are a few questions and considerations to share with your students at the end of the semester:

- Do you know where to find your grade at the end of the semester?

- Take some time to reflect on the overall experience: What worked well for you? What changes do you need to make next time? For example, the amount of time needed to complete assignments.

- Should it stay or should it go? What items do you want or need to keep for later for other classes, practicum, internship, and/or your professional practice? Some items for consideration would be textbooks, references, handouts, PowerPoint presentations, and resources. Suggest to students that they should consider downloading and/or saving these types of files to their computer. They may be helpful later on for professional practice.

- As students copy and save material, keep in mind potential intellectual property and copyright issues.
- Encourage students to provide constructive feedback for the instructor.
- Before the class terminates, suggest that students may want to connect with fellow students/colleagues with whom they want to remain in contact after the class. Request phone numbers, email addresses, and other contact information to remain in contact after the course ends. Within the helping professions, you never know when your colleague will be a potential referral source for one of your students or clients. It is always nice to know there are like-minded colleagues and helpers with whom you can connect professionally within the field. Instructors are unable to share this information after the class due to privacy of personal information and university laws, such as FERPA (Family Educational Rights and Privacy Act). Share this information with students as a teaching moment, but also point out that you are unable to share sensitive personal information given your current role and compliance with university laws.
- Ask the students, what's next for you? Are courses in sequence? Do you need to register for the next course in sequence? Check in with your advisor? Pay tuition? Revisit your plan of study?
- Ask students to share how they will manage the information gained from the course (electronically, paper copies, cloud storage, etc.).
- Celebrate with your students and invite them to relax and embrace the experience! They did it! So celebrate with those you love and enjoy some self-care!

Additional considerations for students: Contacting the instructor may be problematic in the future, as the instructor may not have access to the site and/or may not be employed by the institution when the student wants to retrieve the information.

■ Rules for Students Using the Discussion Boards and Forum

Before the class begins or in the student center in the LMS, we advise sharing rules of etiquette (i.e., netiquette) and user expectations for the discussion boards and forums. Here is a list that we often share with our classes:

1. Post in a scholarly manner when you are responding to a discussion board post for your course. What you write is how you represent yourself to others. How do you want to be known?

2. Avoid spelling, mechanical, and grammatical errors. You can write your response to the discussion board question in a word processing program and then spell-check the document. If you copy and paste your answer

to the discussion board from Microsoft Word, your post will begin with several rows of Word formatting information.

3. If you are asked to cite references to substantiate your response to the discussion board question, do cite your resources correctly using the preferred citation style identified by your instructor (e.g., APA).

4. Research your university's citation builder.

5. Avoid using texting acronyms (e.g., LOL—laughing out loud) in your scholarly response to the discussion board. Such acronyms are best used in an informal environment and do not reflect academic writing. Also, other students in your course may be unfamiliar with these acronyms.

6. Be sure to represent your own ideas when you post. Get informed on plagiarism and copyright infringement. Review the university student conduct and honor code webpages on the university website for more information about violations of the honor code.

7. Follow rules of netiquette when posting to the discussion board. Virginia Shea outlines some of the Core Rules of Netiquette in an excerpt from her book *Netiquette* (www.albion.com/netiquette/corerules.html).

Teach Students How to Communicate with Instructors and Peers

We would love to assume that all our students are well instructed in polite and academic or business communications. Instead of being disappointed, we opt to send our students a guide to professional written communication.

We include the following tips in our guide that we either email to the students or post in the student center.

Spelling and Mechanical Errors

Please spell-check and correct mechanical/grammatical errors. Avoid emails that are written in only lowercase letters. Again, this is a reflection of how you value the correspondence that you are sending and reflects upon your professionalism.

Valedictions or Closings

There are several ways in which you can close an email as you would a letter. For example, "Best," "Best Regards," "Sincerely," "Cordially," and "Yours truly" are all good options.

Email With Your Peers

Your emails with your peers may not be as formal as they are with your instructor, but they should still maintain a respectful attitude and contain all of the elements listed.

It is important for us to remember that our students are coming into the online environment from a variety of backgrounds and situations. Meeting the students where they are and sharing resources in a gentle and compassionate manner models for our students how to set expectations and boundaries in the classroom. Hopefully, this will translate into the students' professional practice as they begin to work with clients.

Sometimes how we share and facilitate the learning process can be just as important, if not more important, than the content we deliver. I always think about Maya Angelou's inspiring quote, "At the end of the day people won't remember what you said or did, they will remember how you made them feel."

How do you want to be remembered after the class is over?

"You can do 99 things for someone and all they'll remember is the one thing you didn't do."—Unknown (livelifehappy.com)

CHAPTER 8

What We've Learned: Tips and Tricks

1. Instructors may be experts in their content area, but everyone brings a unique, authentic worldview into class. What expertise and worldview do you bring into the classroom?

2. What is your worldview? Describe your background, race, ethnicity, sexual orientation, ability, culture, experiences, and so on.

3. How will your worldview influence and affect the way you deliver your content? (Consider ways that your expertise and worldview can be translated into your online classroom.)

4. How will you use your worldview to filter and sift through ways to adapt the content that we share with you throughout the book?

As online instructors, we would like to invite you to consider a few of our perspectives based on our teaching experiences. Ever-changing technology makes us all learners and keeps us continually adding new tools to our teaching "tool belt." We never truly "arrive," but rather are always on a quest to stay current, relevant, and knowledgeable as technology advances.

■ Learning Your LMS and Online Tools

More than likely, someone at your university or even in your department has taught online in the past. Find your resources and technology partners on campus as soon as you can.

As you discover colleagues who have taught online, invite them for a cup of coffee, and ask them to describe their experience with online education. You will benefit from their expertise, knowledge, and support.

Researching New Technology

Before you adopt a new tool, research the technology (tools, apps, programs), and ask colleagues who may have used it before to provide some suggestions, context, and opinions about the technology. Here are some good questions to ask:

- What did you like about the technology?
- What is the learning curve for the instructor and students?
- What training is available? Is it ongoing or one-time training?
- Are there updates?
- What's the cost?
- Does the university support it, and are there any licensing issues?
- Is the cost–benefit worth it?
- Ask your colleague, "Can I sit in on one of your class (i.e., synchronous) sessions?" Or, "Can I view your LMS setup and structure?"
- Would they recommend it to others? Why or why not?

As you explore new tools, consider your student audience and think how and in which classes you would like to implement those tools.

Implementing New Technology

Don't try to implement a ton of different types of technology at the same time in one course. Start small and take baby steps when introducing or trying a new technology. Taking small steps and/or piloting the use of a tool or technology allows you to have a shorter learning curve and less stressful implementation.

Piloting

I was teaching a section of eight students in an introduction to college counseling course in a 15-week semester. I shared with my students in the beginning of the semester that we would be piloting a technology in weeks 14 and 15 of the semester and posted the technology in the learning management system (LMS) for them to play with and explore. I shared training videos for students to review. By waiting until the 15th week of the semester, students had time to build relationships and rapport with one another before trying out something new. For some students, testing out a new technology can be overwhelming and frightening. Knowing this, I made the new technology assignment light-hearted and reflective.

At the end of the semester, I solicited feedback about the tool. Students shared that they enjoyed it, and they thought it would be a nice tool to "shake things up a bit" through the semester compared to the previous semester when they were primarily using discussion forums. My hope was that these students would share their experience with future students in the cohort, and, if the tool was successful, they would teach other students how to use it in the larger cohort section in the summer session.

The pilot program was a success and I adopted the new technology. In the summer session, the eight students were the main trainers for the tool and "helpers" when their colleagues had questions. The students relied on each other when asking questions and as they walked through the technology. I was able to witness increased confidence in my students from their newfound abilities to use and implement this new technology and by sharing content knowledge with their colleagues.

Takeaways

1. Start small and take incremental baby steps when incorporating new technology.
2. Pilot using a smaller class with fewer students, if possible.
3. Offer the technology in a low-stakes scenario (i.e., few points that will not affect the grade in a major way).
4. Allow time for students to develop rapport first, and then offer the technology in the latter part of the semester. This way, students will feel comfortable with each other and help each other work through the technology if there happen to be any technical issues. Believe it or not, these technical issues can be a catalyst for building rapport within a group as they share in this experience together.
5. Ask for feedback from students about their experience engaging with the tools. What did they appreciate? What was challenging for them? What recommendations for implementation, use, or adaptation might they suggest after using the tool in practice?

WORD TO THE WISE: Check your synchronous technology to see what types of files can be uploaded and accepted into the space. Will your LMS work with this new tool? Some systems only will upload PowerPoint slides or a specific version of software. Keep this in mind when preparing your course, especially synchronous sessions. Also, some synchronous platforms allow you to upload content in advance.

▪ Pedagogy and Technology

Don't forget your pedagogy and let "slick" technology entice you. Just because the technology offers a lot of "bells and whistles" does not necessarily mean that your students will learn effectively using it. Your content comes first and the technology should be used only to enhance your course. There are a lot of options out there: be a cautious consumer.

The Multitasking Instructor

In the synchronous online environment, an instructor who can multitask and juggle a variety of activities simultaneously in one space is an asset.

At any one point in class, the instructor may need to manage a PowerPoint presentation on the main board, read student questions and/or sharing in a chat box, and watch for students dropping out and rejoining the session due to technology issues. Also, "moving" students to breakout rooms and back into the main room can take skill. Once students are in the different breakout rooms, the instructor may need to move between rooms to check in on progress—all while typing in the chat box to another breakout room or to the teaching assistant.

While it may feel overwhelming at first, you will learn this skill quickly and soon it will feel as effortless as driving a car. Be patient and take your time the first few sessions; set reasonable expectations for yourself and your students until you are all comfortable with the technology.

WORD TO THE WISE: When possible, it is extremely helpful to have a doctoral student or teaching assistant in the classroom space with you to help you juggle all the activities. As you focus on the structure and content, the doctoral student or teaching assistant can focus on the chat box, move slides, help students who are having technical issues (i.e., logging into the space), and assist with other logistics.

Easy Organization of Cohorts

If you use cohort models and synchronous classrooms, create one session or link per cohort in your platform (e.g., Blackboard Collaborate), instead of creating a separate virtual class for each class you teach in that cohort. This will save you time and reduce confusion for your students. For example, I have one section of Blackboard Collaborate for cohort 1 and all of the classes that I teach in that cohort know to join the session labeled: Dr. Angie Smith's cohort 1 sessions 2015 to 2018.

Weekly Content and Design Organization

As you create your content in your LMS, organize it in a way that is easy to find and navigate. Clearly state directions and expectations for how you plan to manage the space and your overall course.

Build consistency into your weekly design. For example, if you are teaching a 5-week course in the summer, ensure that each week's module looks the same and the headings and fonts are similar week to week. This way, students will easily be able to find information quickly. This consistency helps your class space to "feel" professional and organized.

In some LMSs, instructors can set an "activity completion" function for each activity, link, article, and other assignments within the learning module so that students can indicate with a check mark when they have completed the activity. Students appreciate this "to-do box" function.

WORD TO THE WISE: If you use this feature, be consistent and set up the activity completion function for all required tasks. If you miss one, you will hear about it from the students. In the past, when I have forgotten to set this up, students email, sometimes in a panic, to ensure that I know that they did indeed complete the task, even when the checkmark box was not present.

■ Managing Common Red-Flag Questions From Students

Travel

Student: "I will be traveling during our mandatory synchronous meeting. Is it possible for me to join our session while traveling on the plane?"

No and no. Confidentiality, on so many levels, can be compromised on a plane. In the tight quarters of a plane/train/Uber/cab/Metro, the passenger sitting next to the student will be in eyeshot of the computer screen and all that is occurring in the virtual class space, even if they are unable to hear the session. For obvious reasons, this could be problematic. The same holds true for joining class sessions from a coffee shop, library, restaurant, or other public spaces.

This type of question from students offers the opportunity to link the content covered in our helping professions courses to professional practice, especially around confidentiality, ethics, and privacy.

Just Say No to Cell Phones and Tablets

Student: "Is it OK if I access the class from my cell phone?"

Students may ask to join the class via a cell phone or tablet. We highly recommend against this practice because cell phones and tablets may constrain the student's ability to efficiently operate in the online classroom due to limited interaction with technology used in the class and the small screen size. For example, students on cell phones are unable to use the whiteboard, select emoticons, engage in breakout room activities, use the stylus on the screen to add comments, and so on.

Another obvious reason is the infringement of privacy and confidentiality. We do not know where students are joining us from and who is within earshot of our conversations. Students in the helping professions often share personal and real-life, sometimes even traumatic, experiences that they would not appreciate becoming public. Also, it is important for practitioners-in-training to model confidentiality early on in their careers and begin to actively demonstrate best practices as they segue into a profession that requires confidentiality as a main hallmark.

Ditching Class or Working Ahead

Student: "I am getting married this semester, can I take off 3 weeks for my wedding and honeymoon? Can you open up the learning module a few weeks early so I can work ahead?"

We try to be understanding and accommodating with our busy adult students. However, students can and should be expected to plan ahead. Required courses and required participation are *required*.

Also, changing the course of action or the pace of the class is not possible. In many classes, group work and presentations are part of the course requirements. Missing these experiential opportunities can be detrimental to student learning outcomes. Every student's voice is essential, and when one voice is missing it adversely affects the whole group. It's like the analogy of a choir: when all voices are present and in harmony the sound is beautiful, but when one section or person is missing the melody of the song is compromised. We value everyone's voice in the process throughout the full duration of the semester.

▪ Begin Well

Welcome Letter

Reach out to students before the semester begins. About a week prior to the semester starting, send your class a welcome letter that includes all the information needed to be a successful student in the online course. Share the following information: the systems that will be used; any links; resources; textbook information with a picture of the textbook to reduce questions about editions; dates the course begins; any synchronous meeting times (i.e., schedules); specific requirements for licensure, standards, or accreditation information related to the course; pre-semester work that must be completed; links to tutorials for students who are not familiar with the technology; office hours; contact information for teaching assistant(s); statements about privacy and confidentiality; major project and due dates; passwords needed to access the classroom space; preferred method of communicating with you as the instructor; your contact information; and screenshots of the course homepage.

This may seem like a lot of information to throw at a student—and it is! By sending the letter at least 1 week in advance, you give the students ample time to read it and process it.

Following is the text from a welcome letter from Dr. Angie C. Smith to incoming students:

Dr. Angie C. Smith
Office location
Email address
Date

Dear ECD 524 Online Master's Students/Registrant:

Welcome to ECD 524, Career Counseling! This letter contains procedures and the time schedule for beginning the class.

Our first Blackboard Collaborate (i.e., synchronous) meeting is Monday, May 22, at 8 p.m. Eastern Standard Time (EST).

[*You can also share any teaching assistant contact information and any other relevant information related to logistics for the class.*]

Overview and Textbook

ECD 524 Career Counseling 3 credits

This course is designed to prepare counselors in acquiring the necessary knowledge, skills, and resources needed to provide career counseling to individuals and to design, implement, and evaluate career education and career development programs.

REQUIRED:

Niles, S. G., & Harris-Bowlsbey, J. (2017). *Career development interventions in the 21st century.* (5th ed.). Upper Saddle River, NJ: Pearson. (Note: 4th edition would also be acceptable; only minor revisions between 4th and 5th editions.)

***You can purchase the textbook at the NCSU bookstore, online, or another vendor of your choice.

The syllabus will be available to you on Wednesday, May 17 via Moodle. Moodle will open up on the first day of SUMMER SESSION I on Wednesday, May 17 and we will have our first Blackboard Collaborate meeting in the evening of Monday, May 22 at 8:00 p.m. EST. Can't wait!

Accessing the Course

We will meet in a synchronous setting, meaning all of us will sign on at the same time on Blackboard Collaborate from 8:00 p.m. to 9:30 p.m. EST online.

All of your class information and assignments will be found on and submitted through the LMS. To access it, you must have an Internet connection and a standard web browser.

1. Access to the LMS course site will be granted when classes begin on May 17. You will login to [LMS]. If you have problems logging in, please contact me immediately via my email.

2. For help directly related to the LMS, contact LearnTech by phone or email. For most other issues, including computer-related, Unity ID account, or other general technology questions, contact the university help desk [add help number or help email]. Please feel free to copy me on your help calls, especially as they relate to the LMS, so I can get a sense of the overall issues we encounter. One of my goals is always to have technology facilitate our learning but not get in the way of it; and if there are ever insurmountable technology issues we will work around those issues.

3. As soon as I have information about any "downtimes" for the LMS, I will let you know. All university LMS systems are occasionally taken offline for maintenance. If you are having problems submitting any assignment or completing an activity and can't get to the course website, please let me know.

4. Synchronous "live" sessions: Meetings will take place on Mondays from 8:00 p.m. to 9:30 p.m. EST. To access the site, please visit the following link: [insert your link].

You will need to configure your computer at least 24 hours prior to our meeting.

[Share with students information about tasks that must be completed before joining the course (e.g., any configuration of the computer before logging on to a synchronous session, updating Java or other systems).]

Communication

My primary and preferred mode of communication is email, which I frequently check. If I am going to be away from email more than 24 hours, I will let you know. I usually check email only sporadically on Saturdays and Sundays as that is family time and I am frequently out of the house and away from my email. My hope is that you practice self-care during these times.

Opportunities for Real-Time Interaction

Office Visits

My office is located in the following location: [insert your office location].

I welcome the opportunity to meet you in person. Please feel free to drop by. However, if you have something important to discuss about the class, I suggest you email ahead of time so we can schedule an appointment. I also encourage students to meet with me through phone conversations, Skype, Google Hangouts, and our online synchronous system.

I know this letter contains a lot of information! Please contact me at my email address at any time if you have questions. I look forward to our work together this semester! "See" you soon!

Best wishes,

Angie C. Smith

[Include your email address]

Instructors should remember that students may need to configure their computers by a specified time frame, such as 24 hours in advance of the class starting. Give the students specific instructions about how to access the LMS and synchronous platforms used for "live" sessions. Also, share any technical support numbers and emails.

Additionally, share with students the procedure they should follow in the event that they experience technical issues logging on to the systems. Request that students email you and/or your teaching assistant to communicate with you that they are experiencing problems, as well. You may have experienced the issue before and be able help to remedy it. It is also nice to know that students are continuing to attempt to log in and not just skipping class.

Asynchronous Introductions

As a way of introduction in an asynchronous environment, ask the students to respond to the following prompt:

"Welcome! Please introduce yourself to your classmates. In the spirit of career counseling, please provide some brief background about how you came to the mental health field. Also, share your first job that you can remember and whether or not you enjoyed it. Why or why not?" Another adaptation could be to ask students to describe a job or career they would never want to engage in during their lives; then ask students why. Describe to students how learning more about the aspects in their lives that they do not enjoy can lead to deeper revelations about what they do enjoy.

A similar method of introductions in the asynchronous environment is to ask students to provide their preferred name as well as something about themselves that will help the instructor and their colleagues remember them. Students are reminded to use appropriate self-disclosure in revealing things that make them memorable, but the answers are just that—memorable! One of my students fostered a rare breed of dog, another was having a baby that semester, others were getting married, another spoke five languages. I was the only one who had been skydiving! It is important to share a memorable thing about yourself and model the type of disclosure that would be appropriate.

Relationship and Communication

Information Sharing

Reflect on the types of relationships you want to have with your students over time, and consider the type and amount of information you decide to share with them. For example, if you are going to be out of town for a conference, it is important to share this type of information so they will be aware of your availability. If you will be joining a class session from a remote location or one where there may be connectivity issues, it can be helpful to share with your students this information in advance in the event that you are kicked out of the "live" session unexpectedly. Students will appreciate knowing you are in a location that may be experiencing technical difficulties for a valid reason.

Keep Them Updated

Send announcements to students with updates and any changes to the syllabus, content, assignments, or your availability. Also, send students emails summarizing your thoughts after grading an assignment and with encouraging emails to stay engaged with students during the week.

Attendance

Students may request to miss a synchronous session due to a special event, child's orientation, anniversary, birthday, and/or other celebratory events. Prior to teaching online, consider how you will handle these requests. Will you permit students to miss a specific number of classes per semester? Will you permit students to watch a recording of the "live" session?

WORD TO THE WISE: In some instances, the instructor can handle excused absences by allowing students to watch the video of the live session and then create a one-page document or 3-minute video highlighting either three points they would have shared if they had attended the session or three elements of the class session that they found interesting and useful for their professional development or future practice. Adult students sometimes need to miss for professional development opportunities, conferences, work engagements, and so on, and offering ways to make up the work is often appreciated and unexpected.

Attending Class on the Road

As the instructor, when I am traveling to conferences or on vacation, I take a picture or a short video of where I am staying to share with the students. During the synchronous session, I sometimes turn the camera on the building or location where I am teaching from to share the experience with my class. I encourage students to do the same and share their experiences as they travel. We have had students join synchronous sessions from all over the world. Sharing these images creates another opportunity to share our lives together, build community, and better understand cross-cultural experiences.

■ Response Time

Emails

Reflect on your preference for responding to email: What meets your comfort level? Set boundaries that are appropriate and work for you. For example, share with students that you will not be responding to emails during the weekends, or set days/times when you do and do not respond to your email. As we know, responding to email can be a 24/7 job! As instructors, we want to set the tone and expectation so that everyone is on the same page. We can intentionally link this back to self-care and best practices within the helping professions, especially the need to avoid burnout.

A nice touch to close an email is for the instructor to tell the students, "I will 'see' you later," on the designated evening for a synchronous session. I put quotation marks around "see" due to the nature of our "live" sessions where we will not physically be with each other but we will virtually see everyone who is in the same space with us. I have found that students have modeled the same language in their return emails with me.

Connecting With Students Outside of the Class

Because technology is so pervasive, students often will ask to "friend" us on Facebook, LinkedIn, or other social media outlets. Consider your ethical codes and standards of practice and model the appropriate actions when working with your students. They will learn from you based on what you do and how you respond. Also, consider the implications of connecting with students while they are still participating in your program.

Peer Feedback

When possible, it is great to provide opportunities for students to share and learn with each other. For example, one assignment in a career development course that I taught requires students to complete their resume for the course. After completing the resume, they are to locate a partner, trade resumes, and provide concrete feedback for peer review. This helps them build better resumes; also, learning how to provide critical feedback relates to students' professional growth and development, which is essential to the helping professions. How can you incorporate peer review and feedback into your online course(s)?

◼ Experiential Learning: Practicum, Internships, and Beyond

Students who are training in the helping professionals typically are required to engage in an experiential on-site interaction with clients. University and site supervisors guide the students' learning and offer feedback about student skills, professional practice, and client cases. Working in an online environment, practicum, internship, and supervisory experiences take on a different framework. Students practice skills at their preferred site in person and receive online supervision via video technology such as VSee or other confidential sites that do not compromise client information and data. VSee connects students in peer or individual supervision with their university instructor. It creates a visual and audio connection with participants so they may share content and view nonverbal language between the instructor and the students.

For another layer of security, students in the helping professions can share with their clients that there will be online supervision with their university instructor. Then a confidentiality waiver is signed by the student to ensure that everyone is on the same page.

WORD TO THE WISE: Prior to the start of supervision, the instructor should set expectations and parameters for conducting online supervision. The instructor-supervisor needs to relay to everyone involved the importance of joining the supervisory sessions from a private, solitary space that is enclosed and free from distractions, noise, and possible interruptions. It is vital that there are no privacy violations with any client information that is communicated during the supervisory sessions.

Dyad-Client Intake Exercise

The dyad-client exercise gives online students the opportunity to experience and practice a client relationship and activity. Divide students into dyads and provide the following information before sending a small group to breakout rooms. One common activity within the helping professions is to conduct a client intake to learn more about our client's background, experience, presenting issues, goals, and so on. Instructors can create or include an actual form in the LMS to complete prior to the synchronous session. For this exercise, students are asked to simulate a fictitious client story, if so desired. Create a slide including the following questions:

1. What brings you in today?
2. What is your most pressing issue at this time?
3. What do you hope to get out of this work? How is it different from what you would do on your own?
4. Tell me something about yourself that you think would be important for me to know as your social worker, psychologist, counselor, or other helping professional.

Share with students that this is not to serve as an actual therapy session, but rather an opportunity to practice skills in a "live" environment in preparation for joining the field. At any point during the experience, if students become uncomfortable with the activity, they can remove themselves from the session.

Once in the breakout room, ask students to determine who will serve in the roles of the helping professional and client, then ask them to practice conducting an intake interview with one another. Allow about 5 minutes for the first round, and then have students switch roles so that both students can experience the client role and the helping professional role. Set the timer in the synchronous environment and send an announcement when the timer goes off to ask students to switch roles. As students are practicing, move around to each of the breakrooms to answer questions and observe the sessions. Instructors can elect to use only audio sessions or incorporate video elements as well for the intake activity.

After 10 minutes, bring all students back together in the main space and reflect on the experience. Ask the following questions:

1. What was this experience like for you?
2. What did you learn about serving in the helping professional role?
3. How was the experience as a client? As the counselor?
4. As you consider joining the helping professions, what will you take with you from this experience that will help you to effectively engage in an intake interview with your future clients?
5. Anything else you want to share?

■ Design

Play!

As you are learning and designing your course in your LMS, take time to play with all the tools and functions, and even create a designated play space where you can add and delete content, practice using the technology, press buttons, try out features, and so on.

You can also create your courses in this play space, and then copy the content over to the course site each semester. As the semester progresses, any changes, adaptations, and so forth that you make to the course can be added to the play space as you go, and then be included in future courses.

Creating a Visually Appealing Course Design

When designing an asynchronous course, don't forget about the aesthetics, visual appeal, and inviting images to evoke positive reactions. Consider how you can bring soothing and calming colors into your course, as students will be spending a lot of time in this space. Developing a welcoming space where students enjoy spending time throughout the week is really important.

WORD TO THE WISE: When I created a group counseling course, I applied for a grant to support my course development. When discussing the course with the instructional designers, I told them that my goal was to create a calming, inviting, relaxing space. The images we decided to use in the banners were similar to images used in helping professionals' websites: water, rocks, and soothing colors. (For more information about the course, see Chapter 12.)

Syllabus Quiz

Encourage deep reading of the syllabus by giving a quiz. The quiz can be Q&A or multiple choice. Ask questions about main ideas that are often missed. This cuts down on syllabus-related class time questions and emails. The LMS can even be pre-populated to grade the quiz automatically.

Linking

In asynchronous environments, as you create your course shell, link the learning objectives back to the syllabus as well as course outline/structure to assist students in navigating the asynchronous space easily. Creating synergy among the course objectives, course outline, and learning objectives is essential.

Friendly reminder: Check out Bloom's Taxonomy for more information. Another great resource is *A Taxonomy for Learning, Teaching and Assessing: A Revision of Bloom's Taxonomy of Educational Objectives*, edited by L. W. Anderson and D. R. Krathwohl.

Use Quotes and Images

Adding inspirational and related quotes and pictures to capture a concept or idea can help students solidify main points and make connections from the "real world" to the helping professions. When sending announcements and notes to students, after the closing of the email, include a picture, quote, encouraging word, or other positive affirmation to brighten the email and their day.

Assessment and Testing

Evaluating students in the online classroom can be accomplished in all the usual ways—quizzes, tests, projects, and other assignments—via the LMS, on-site at the university, and through proctor services. It is important for instructors to detail, at the beginning of the semester, the expectations and methods used for testing so students can be prepared.

On-site testing centers: Universities typically offer an on-site testing center for students to complete tests on site in a given time period. Instructors can work with university testing centers to plan and schedule the logistics of the testing for students in the course.

Proctors: Instructors can explore the proctor services offered at their institution. Seeking specific information about the process for scheduling proctors for on-site testing and other services could be a lifesaver when offering tests for a course.

LMS tests: Instructors can create tests that are offered on the LMS, including timed tests for multiple-choice or short answers. Short quizzes with 10 or fewer questions that are low stakes work great as student "check-ins" to ensure that students are reading the content.

Asynchronous Student Center

In some LMSs (e.g., Moodle), instructors can create a "book" and build items to share with students about expectations, guidelines, and helpful tips for successfully navigating the course. A few items to include in the online "book" for "getting started" may include:

1. Welcome letter and/or picture/video introduction of the instructor
2. Course overview
3. About the instructor
4. Resources specific for the course
5. Cyber café or student lounge for sharing and connecting with one another
6. How to prepare for a synchronous meeting (instructions for setup using technology)
7. Office hours (in-person and/or virtual) and communication preferences
8. Technologies to be used in the course
9. Plug-ins needed
10. Configuration directions for the computer
11. Netiquette (i.e., rules for online communication)
12. Sample message of how to communicate effectively and ineffectively with instructor(s)
13. Discussion tips for communicating in forums
14. Summary and excitement about starting the course

Cyber Café or Student Lounge

Like many instructors, I like to build a student lounge or cyber café to provide an opportunity for students to interact without me. It is a student-only place that I do not monitor, but I do ask students to let me know if I need to check in. There have been instances in the past where a few undergraduates had a disagreement—exactly like in a real student lounge! The guidelines for using the café are listed in the syllabus and in the forum and read: This space is for student discussion. It is not monitored by the instructor(s). If you would like to all plan a 5K or want to talk about the newest/hottest television series, you can do it here. This space is for you to discuss non–course-related things that tickle your fancy.

Scaffolding Large Assignments

Instructors can use scaffolding to break large assignments into manageable parts. Instructors can assign specific due dates for each part. Each part of the assignment can stand alone or they can build on one another. The instructor can offer low-stakes opportunities for students to demonstrate competency early on in the process and then build upon what they learned. By the end of the semester, students are surprised by how nicely the components fit together.[1]

Templates

Spend time creating template documents for specific activities and tasks. Any document that you tend to use or send out over and over again is a great candidate for a template document. You can reuse and change the dates on these templates with little effort and maximize efficiency as well as productivity.

How to Get Guest Speakers Into Your Classroom

Just because you are moving your content online doesn't mean that you can't have guests! Invite your guest speakers to join the synchronous space to share their knowledge, background, and tips from the field. Students are so impressed to be sitting in their own home while learning from experts in the field.

I wanted to invite documentary filmmakers who were attending an on-campus function to present their film to my online class. So, I reached out to the contact person who arranged the on-campus meeting, and she provided the contact information for me to call the presenters. After talking with the presenter, she indicated that both the film creators and the moderator would be able to attend my online class. They were very excited to use this platform to share their story.

Here are the steps I took to make this presentation happen:

- I contacted the presenters about 1 month prior to the guest presentation.
- The documentary had a specific cost associated with it. I reached out to my department head to secure funding to purchase the link to add to the

[1] A great resource for scaffolding is E-learning Faculty Modules: elearningfacultymodules .org/index.php/Scaffolding_Learning_for_Novices,_Amateurs,_and_Experts

course for students to view at their leisure in the LMS prior to the guest speaker's arrival.

- I shared the class size, format, technology, class link and password, and other logistics with the presenters. I sent them directions for navigating the online platform and sent them my contact information in case they experienced any issue. I recommended that they "arrive" about 15 minutes prior to the class starting, so we could work through any last-minute technical issues.

- About 1 month prior to the guest speakers' visit, I announced to students that there would be three presenters sharing in our online space. I encouraged students to be welcoming and engaging.

- I required students to view the documentary that I had linked on the LMS.

- I created a Google Doc and uploaded it to the LMS. In the document, students shared any questions that they had for the presenters. I gave students 1 week to write down their questions, and then I shared this document with the presenter.

- One week before the presentation, I tested the technology with our guest speakers to ensure that they were able to configure their computers and log into the system.

- As the presenters joined the space, I introduced them to the students and facilitated the discussion.

- After the session, I followed up with the presenters to thank them for their time, expertise, and energy. The day after the presentation, I emailed them the positive comments and feedback I received from my students.

WORD TO THE WISE: Before guest speakers join the session, be sure to coordinate the technology with them to provide access to the space, including any passcodes that are needed for them to join the session. If possible, test the technology prior to the session with the guest speaker.

Lectures

Let's redefine the use of lectures. In our synchronous spaces (i.e., live interactions online), instructors are urged to create classes that encourage students to explore and engage in activities, case studies, discussion, and so on, rather than simply listening to or watching an hour lecture about a specific topic.

Mini-lectures or "lecturettes" can be prerecorded and uploaded to the LMS for the students to watch before a synchronous class session, and then students can attend the synchronous space to discuss, practice, and present information to one another about the content. To ensure that the students actually watch the recordings, instructors can create a short quiz, discussion forum prompt, or journal reflection. These types of activities can ensure that students will read and engage with the material.

Lecturettes can be useful in asynchronous courses. They may provide extra guidance for students as they embark on learning. The instructor can create a lecturette (a 4- to 7-minute long video) each week to outline or highlight the important terms and major takeaways for students to take note of as they complete the course readings and engage with the information in the learning module.

Breakout Rooms

In asynchronous and synchronous platforms, breakout rooms can enhance group work and collaboration among students. In synchronous environments, instructors can present a concept or case study, randomly assign small groups of students to breakout rooms, and move them to their appropriate rooms. In the breakout rooms, students can only see and/or hear what is happening in their breakout room. In this space, students can view slides, use the white-board, add content, and share information on the screen. The instructor can set the timer for a specified amount of time for students to work on the case, assignment, or whatever, and then bring all the students back to the main room for a large-group discussion. Additionally, instructors can copy all whiteboards from the breakout rooms into the main room and ask student groups to report on what they learned or discovered while in the breakout room.

Group Work

There are several ways to develop groups in your online class. You can create groups based on what you know about your students, which works well in a cohort model where you get to know your students over a course of time. They can also be established by strengths of the students, expertise in a specific content area, life experiences, and developmental life phases (e.g., students who are all of the same age, which can have its advantages and drawbacks). In some instances, creating groups that are heterogeneous can be beneficial to ensure that there is a diversification of ideas, experiences, and skill sets.

The instructor may also invite students to participate in the formation of groups. In an asynchronous environment, there are poll features where students can choose their preferred date to present, turn in group work, or select group participants. Instructors can set perimeters such as "Group 1 and presentation date, Group 2 and presentation date," and limit of the number of students in each group. When a group or date is full, students must select a different group.

One potential issue with this method is that students who take initiative and are eager to review the content in the LMS often secure the best (i.e., latest) times and dates first. Concurrently, students who join the course late or who are less passionate about the course may be left with the early dates to present or turn in their work. This is the way life goes sometimes; "the early bird gets the worm."

The value of letting students select their own groups is that they become even more vested in their experience when they get to pick their own due dates and partners for group projects. Students feel like they are part of the planning process, rather than being assigned partners with whom they may not feel comfortable working on a project. Also, adult learners are busy, and providing them with the freedom of selection can help them take ownership of their own experience and calendar.

There are also limits to group work as well, including timelines, schedules, attentiveness to the task at hand from group members, looming deadlines, confidentiality of content and personal information of all participants or group members. Students may push back on group work in online classes just as they do in on-campus courses. However, encourage students to explore ways to enhance their learning with their peers and community.

Group work redefined: To facilitate good group work, offer students resources that will help them connect and work efficiently. Broaden your scope around the group work experience by using conference calls, email, Skype, WebEx, Google Docs, meeting online before or after synchronous sessions, breakout rooms, Schriver, . . . the list goes on and on.

Video Production

In recording or screencasting videos, keep the length to a minimum of 3 minutes but no more than 15 to 20 minutes. Think about your own attention span and how long you would be interested in watching a video online. Typically, there are distractions that prevent us from viewing a long video in its entirety. Keeping the content and video engaging is essential to keeping your students' attention, building community, and relating well with your students.

WORD TO THE WISE: When uploading the video, add a label with the title of the video clip and in parentheses add the duration of the video (e.g., Lecture 1, 3 minutes).

Student Presentations

One assignment that can be linked to group work is student presentations. Students are given the opportunity to select a partner and date to present on a specific topic related to the course. In the past, I have shared examples, with permission, from former students as a model for the structure and logistics that I expect. In some cases, sharing a recording as a link in the asynchronous space (i.e., the LMS) can be an additional option for students to view examples.

WORD TO THE WISE: To continue to connect and build rapport with your students, send a follow-up email after student presentations in the online synchronous space to let them know their work is valued and that you appreciate the way they handled the online presentation. Students appreciate this additional layer of connection, encouragement, and support.

Logistics of Student Presentations

In an on-campus class, student presentations consist of plugging a flash drive into the classroom computer, signing into an email account and opening a file, or retrieving a presentation document through the cloud or Google account. After the student retrieves the file, the student simply projects the file on a screen and begins progressing through the presentation. In an online environment, the instructor takes on a more active role in this process.

Here are some of the possible steps to be taken prior to a student presentation:

• The student uploads the presentation to the asynchronous private or public link within the LMS.

• The instructor retrieves the file, and saves it in a secure location on the computer.

• At some point prior to the synchronous session, the instructor uploads the file to the synchronous space for the student.

WORD TO THE WISE: As an instructor, share with students that they are responsible for the content and that the ability to use technology effectively will not be a part of their grade. Sometimes students can be very anxious that their grade will be linked to the success and effectiveness in demonstrating the use of technology, which is typically not the case in presentations within the helping professions. During the presentations, the instructor can work behind the scenes to advance the slides for the student presenters; copy and paste URLs, articles, links, resources, and other items that the student shares with the group; help with application sharing; facilitate any polls; and move students into breakout rooms if the presenting student chooses to use this option.

Pecha Kucha for Speedy Presentations: www.pechakucha.org

For student presentations, instructors can require that students use the Pecha Kucha method whereby students present material and content in a concise, organized, and speedy fashion. Presenters share roughly 20 slides in a total of 6 minutes. That means each slide must be explained in about 20 seconds. This allows instructors to have 20 students make presentations in one evening. Instructors can use the Pecha Kucha method for quick reviews of chapter materials and content that can easily be digested in limited time frames.

Synchronous courses: Instructors can upload the Pecha Kucha slides to the "live" space and students can present the material in "real time."

Asynchronous courses: Require students to create a Pecha Kucha presentation, record their presentation on video, and upload it to a private YouTube link. Once the YouTube link is created, students can copy and paste it into the LMS for peer and instructor viewing and grading.

Prezi for Asynchronous Presentations: www.Prezi.com
The Prezi presentation format allows students to create presentations that have myriad multimedia tools embedded. Students can embed charts, graphs, citations, video clips, recordings, and more in their presentations.

WORD TO THE WISE: Check to see what types of files can be uploaded and are accepted by your synchronous technology. Some systems only will upload

PowerPoint slides or a specific version of software. Keep this in mind when preparing your course, especially synchronous sessions. Also, some synchronous platforms allow content to be uploaded in advance.

While teaching a class on social policy using the HBO series *The Wire*, I asked students to create a Prezi concept map that demonstrated the interactions and connections of social problems as reflected in *The Wire* and in course readings. One student created a concept map that has had more than 35,000 views on Prezi. The link for these presentations can also be uploaded to the LMS and shared with peers.

1 Second Everyday: www.1se.co
The 1 Second Everyday app can be used to track progress for students over the course of the semester. Students can capture a picture or idea for 1 second each day throughout the course of the semester as a means of reflecting on how much they have grown in their skills, knowledge in the field, and content area.

WORD TO THE WISE: The app can also be used within the helping professions with our clients. Therapists could use the app with clients for capturing a short time period and tracking progress, goals, and so on over time.

■ Engagement and Interactivity

Managing After-Class Engagement

In a synchronous classroom setting, students may want to talk about the content or simply connect about life in general after the class is over for the day. Sometimes, I stay in the online, synchronous space and invite students to stay and ask questions for 5 to 10 minutes after class. If students want to talk about group work, I move them into their own breakout rooms to discuss in private.

Sometimes students just want to catch up and chat after class, similar to an on-campus class. I tell the students that they can remain in the space for as long as they would like and I will not be recording it, but I will not be online. I step away from the computer, but leave the session open so they can continue to talk.

Managing In-Class Participation

One concern of many online instructors is the lack of participation or engagement in the synchronous classroom. I like to check in on students to make sure they haven't checked out of the classroom, either cognitively or physically. I post impromptu polling questions for students to respond to. For example, in the middle of a session, I may ask students to select an emoticon or check mark to indicate that they are still "with me." I can visually see who quickly responds, or not. For students who routinely neglect to make a selection, I (or my TA) send a private message to ask how they are doing, if we can provide clarity around the topic, or if there is anything that is prohibiting them from participating. These periodic, random check-ins act as a mid-class roll call that keeps students engaged who may otherwise drift off.

Also, students may inadvertently be "kicked out" of a synchronous session and unable to answer the poll. Be sure to share with students in the first class that if they get kicked out, it's OK. Simply log back in and rejoin class. As the student rejoins and enters the space, welcome the student in the chat box and check in with that person. Students appreciate that you noticed that they were missing. You also can provide technical or other support, as needed.

Managing Student Conversations

Consider treating discussion boards like seated class meetings. Some students have to be prompted to contribute and others dominate the conversation. I modified a tool I learned from another instructor that uses roles for student participation. I used this tool in an online social policy class that viewed the HBO series *The Wire*. *The Wire* has five seasons and 2 weeks of discussion and readings are devoted to each season. I set up a schedule for participation and assigned each student a role for the first week. The weeks then rotated.

Here's how it works: Each student is assigned a role so that not every student is posting at the same time, and each group of students has a specific task for that season. The roles and responsibilities are:

The First Writers post initial questions and insights about the season's material to the class blog the first week.

The Respondents disagree with or clarify the First Writers' posts.

The Searchers find and share at least one relevant online resource and provide a short evaluation of the resource, highlighting what makes it worthwhile, unusual, or problematic.

The Breathers are students who do not have to contribute to the blog. They can take the week off.

The roles for each student are assigned during the first season of the series and rotate with each season. If or when all the students are readily engaged and everyone is actively participating, then the roles are no longer necessary and no longer assigned. I also tell my students that they do not have to stay in their roles. As long as they fulfill their role in class, they can take on another one too.

Avoid Overengagement

If you are offering a synchronous or hybrid class where you are meeting in person or "live," in addition to using a discussion forum (such as Voicethread), you may want to monitor how frequently you are asking students to share and engage. Overengagement can hinder the learning process and cause students to feel overwhelmed with the amount they are required to reflect, share, and engage with one another in addition to the work that is being required from the asynchronous environment. We want to develop good listeners, but we don't want to flood them by oversharing, particularly learners who prefer more of a solitary learning environment. Definitely keep your students and their various preferred learning styles in mind when implementing and offering engagement opportunities.

■ Managing and Encouraging Student Initiative

Student Initiative

Students need to take initiative. The nature of online learning involves student buy-in and investment in the process. Students may be under the assumption that the instructor is going to perform all the work—but this is inaccurate. Online students are not passive learners; they should be actively engaged in their learning. When the instructor shares due dates, rubrics, and specific course requirements, it helps students know how they will be evaluated in the course and sparks initiative.

Values Assessments

Within the helping professions, incorporating a reflective exercise related to values and value exploration is part of the student journey to self-awareness of who they are as helping professionals. Value assessments used in the classroom can then be transferred into the students' work in the future within field placement, experiential learning opportunities, practicum, internship, and full-time employment with clients.

The Good Project website offers a click-and-drag values sorting chart that is a good tool for online courses (thegoodproject.org/toolkits-curricula/the-goodwork-toolkit/value-sort-activity).

The Life Values Inventory is a free values assessment for students to explore as well (www.lifevaluesinventory.org/index.html).

Interest Assessments

Give students the opportunity to learn more about themselves and their interests. John Holland's theory of career assessment[2] is a quick assessment that can be completed in a synchronous session and then discussed as a whole group. In career counseling classes, this assessment can be offered as an instrument to use with their clients in the future.

Mindfulness

Mindfulness exercises, such as a guided meditation or relaxation technique, can be fun and helpful things to add to learning modules. Mindfulness exercises benefit students personally and prepare them to enter the asynchronous space to complete their work after perhaps a hectic day. Also, role modeling and demonstrating mindfulness techniques can be learned by students based on the techniques selected. Instructors can create and guide their own meditation and mindfulness exercise designed for the students, whereby students hear the instructor's voice and follow prompts. The instructor can also add relaxation,

---

[2] RIASEC Test; uhcc.hawaii.edu/jobcenter/riasec_multiLang.php

mindfulness, or meditation tips or pictures to the asynchronous space. There are tons of online resources that can be linked to in the beginning of each module.

WORD TO THE WISE: Share how you are going to present the mindfulness information and how the mindfulness exercise will be used, linking the course content to professional as well as personal development.

Developing Professional Identity

In an asynchronous environment, invite your students to research the professional associations, organizations, networks, ethical standards websites, listservs, and potential local, state, national, and international connections that are on offer in the helping professions. Students can create and add to a central discussion post, to Pinterest, or to a single Google Doc to create a class list to take with them after the course is over.

After students identify the URL and web links, ask students to identify three pieces of data on the site that relates to their interests, professional goals, and/or opportunities to explore now and in the future.

A few websites that may be useful to explore within the helping professions follow.

Psychology

American Educational Research Association: www.aera.net
American Psychological Association: www.apa.org
Association for Psychological Sciences: www.psychologicalscience.org
Ethical Principles of Psychologists and Code of Conduct: www.apa.org/ethics/code
European Association for Research on Learning and Instruction: www.earli.org
The National Association for Multicultural Education: www.nameorg.org
Society for Personality and Social Psychology: www.spsp.org

Marriage and Family Therapy

American Association for Marriage and Family Therapy: www.aamft.org/iMIS15/AAMFT
American Association for Marriage and Family Therapy Code of Ethics: www.aamft.org/iMIS15/AAMFT/Content/Legal_Ethics/Code_of_Ethics.aspx
American Family Therapy Academy: www.afta.org
Commission on Accreditation for Marriage and Family Therapy Education: www.coamfte.org/iMIS15/coamfte
European Family Therapy Association: www.europeanfamilytherapy.eu
International Association of Marriage and Family Counselors: www.iamfc.org
International Family Therapy Association: www.ifta-familytherapy.org
National Council on Family Relations: www.ncfr.org

Counseling

American Art Therapy Association: arttherapy.org
American College Counseling Association: www.collegecounseling.org
American Counseling Association: www.counseling.org
American Mental Health Counselors Association: www.amhca.org/home
American School Counselor Association: www.schoolcounselor.org
Association for Counselor Education and Supervision: www.acesonline.net
Chi Sigma Iota (Counseling Academic & Professional Honor Society International): www.csi-net.org
Council for Accreditation of Counseling and Related Educational Programs: www.cacrep.org
International Association of Counseling Services: iacsinc.org/home.html
National Board for Certified Counselors: www.nbcc.org
National Career Development Association: www.ncda.org/aws/NCDA/pt/sp/home_page
National Employment Counseling Association: www.employmentcounseling.org
Society of Counseling Psychology: www.div17.org

Social Work

American Board of Examiners in Clinical Social Work: www.abecsw.org
American Case Management Association: www.acmaweb.org
Association for Gerontology Education in Social Work: www.agesocialwork.org
Association of Social Work Boards: www.aswb.org
Clinical Social Work Association: www.clinicalsocialworkassociation.org
Council on Social Work Education: www.cswe.org
National Association of Black Social Workers: nabsw.org
National Association of Social Workers: www.socialworkers.org/pubs/code/default.asp
National Hospice and Palliative Care Organization: www.nhpco.org
The Network for Social Work Management: socialworkmanager.org
School Social Work Association of America: www.sswaa.org
Society for Social Work and Research: www.sswr.org

Gerontology

American Geriatrics Society: www.americangeriatrics.org
American Society on Aging: www.asaging.org
The Gerontological Society of America:www.geron.org
National Association for Professional Gerontologists: www.napgerontologists.org
National Council on Aging: www.ncoa.org

Higher Education and Student Affairs

American Academics and Higher Education: www.aahe.org
American Association of Colleges for Teacher Education: www.aacte.org

The American Association of Collegiate Registrars and Admissions Officers: www.aacrao.org

American Association of Community Colleges: www.aacc.nche.edu/Pages/default.aspx

American Association of University Professors: www.aaup.org

American College Personnel Association: www.myacpa.org/ethics

American Educational Research Association: www.aera.net/divisions/j

Association of American Universities: www.aau.edu

Association of Governing Boards of Universities and Colleges: www.agb.org

National Association of Student Personnel and Administrators: www.naspa.org

National Education Association: www.nea.org/home/1602.htm

The School Superintendents Association: www.aasa.org

Community in Cohorts

An easy way to build community in a cohort model is to create a social committee to coordinate activities outside the classroom. If there are multiple cohorts, connecting leaders from each cohort into a committee to plan events can be useful and yield more participation. To do this, the instructor invites students to create a social committee (two to three students per cohort) and sets the perimeters and expectations for the group. Share with students that the social events are not required and completely optional, as they are not connected to the courses or grades in any way. It is OK to miss the social events—there is no obligation to attend. Instructors can decide to attend the events as well. Students appreciate seeing faculty in this setting.

The students on the committee plan and brainstorm ideas for the social events. A student who is a yoga instructor may invite the class to group yoga classes to practice self-care throughout the semester. Some of the events the social committee has planned are yoga sessions, self-defense trainings, hiking at local parks, gathering at local restaurants, art therapy workshops, and the like. Virtual social events could also be part of the mix. Students are so creative and become vested and interested in participating when they are a part of the planning process.

▪ Grades and Grading

Lighten Your Grading Load

Offer intervals or date ranges for students to upload their finished assignments to the LMS. Typically, the overachievers will turn in assignments early, and there are always students who wait until the last minute to turn things in. The interval system also allows students to plan ahead and schedule accordingly based on their own life obligations, projects, schedules, and other constraints.

Use Rubrics

The use of grading rubrics for assignments and presentations helps students know and understand the expectations prior to turning in work. Before the semester begins, develop rubrics and build automatic grading forms. Built-in rubrics in the LMS can save you time later when assignments are turned in from students.

At the end of this chapter, we offer you resources for creating rubrics for your class. Table 8.1 is a sample rubric from a career counseling class taught to graduate level students offered online asynchronously and synchronously.

Table 8.1 Sample rubric: theory handout rubric.

Criteria	Limited Proficiency	Satisfactory	Exemplary	Weight
History of the theory	Described little to no history of the theory	Provided several key elements of the theory from a historical perspective	Clearly highlighted the history of the theory, including details and examples	10
Summary of major tenets of the theory	Little to no summary of the tenets of the theory	Moderately summarized the major tenets, including one or two details	Thoroughly summarized the major tenets of the theory	10
Recommended populations	No reference of the recommended populations	Briefly described the recommended populations	Clearly articulated the recommended populations	10
Cultural implications	Little to no reference of cultural implications	Briefly described cultural implications	Thoroughly described cultural implications and provided details	10
Gaps in the theory	No mention of the gaps in the theory	Adequately shared the gaps in the theory	Provided a detailed explanation of the gaps in the theory	5
Five to six peer-reviewed references	Zero to two peer-reviewed journals referenced	Three to four peer-reviewed journals referenced	Five to six peer-reviewed journals referenced	5

Example: Mock Crisis Intervention Session Rubric

In my mock crisis intervention session assignment, pairs of students conduct mock sessions as client and counselor. Students are required to use technology (e.g., phone, web conferencing) to complete the assignment. Then students describe and reflect on their experiences using the criteria listed in Table 8.2.

Grades and Returning Graded Assignments

Set up a system to grade papers, presentation, and other assignments. A rule of thumb is to set the expectation with students about your plan in grading their papers and when you anticipate returning the grades—a week is typical. Obviously, this depends on the length of the semester and assignment. Longer assignments may take extended time to grade and provide thoughtful feedback.

Table 8.2 Mock crisis rubric.

60 Points Possible	High Mastery
Up to 30 points (10 points each)	*Mock counselor* Description of the presenting problem. Description of the model of crisis intervention used is provided and how each step of the model was implemented. Description of the suicide assessment. *Mock client* An overview of the session is provided including a description of the presenting problem. Description of thoughts and feelings experienced during the session (in general). Description of thoughts and feelings during suicide assessment.
Up to 20 points	*Mock counselor* What personal qualities or characteristics (as recognized in this particular session) might enhance or impede your ability to be an effective crisis worker? *Mock client* How might the crisis experience (as described in this particular session) increase the potential for countertransference when working with clients who have experienced similar forms of trauma and crisis?
Up to 5 points	Summation is clear, concise, and thorough, with few spelling, punctuation, or grammar errors
Up to 5 points	Summation is at least 300 words in length and no more than 500

WORD TO THE WISE: Set expectations around when you plan on returning graded assignments to the students to reduce their anxiety and the resulting abundance of email inquiries. Also, if you are teaching multiple classes, cross-check your calendar to make sure that you are not scheduling due dates for both classes at the same time.

▪ Advising: Efficiency and Streamlining Online

One tactic to efficiently advise students who are enrolled in a cohort model is to create a Google Doc offering several dates for all advisees of the cohort to attend after the synchronous class session. The students who are not part of the instructor's advisee load exit the class before the meeting begins. Advisees often have the same questions, and they learn from questions they may not have even considered. After the group session, I offer individual sessions to advisees who have specific questions related to their situation that they want to share in confidence.

The following is a form advisee letter (created in Google Doc) that includes radio buttons to allow students to select specific dates for preferred synchronous advising sessions with the instructor.

Dr. Angie Smith's Advising Letter to Cohort Advisees

RE: Dr. Angie Smith's College Counseling Advising Sessions (Summer and Fall 2017)

Please read the email below and select whether or not you will be able to attend the advising session for your cohort. All sessions will be held in Blackboard Collaborate under "Dr. Angie Smith's 2016 to 2019 sessions" from 9:30 p.m. to 10:00 p.m. EST. Looking forward to "seeing" everyone online soon! Please review the course plan document that includes your class schedule for your cohort in the 3-year period in preparation for our meeting. Looking forward to it!

Subject line: Welcome to [College Counseling Advisement]!

Greetings, [College Counseling majors],

I hope this note finds you doing well! It's hard to believe, but we have arrived at the point for advising for the Summer and Fall 2017 semesters. You may have already registered for the summer courses last year, which is fine, since the sequence of course offerings are standard and routine for your cohort. I just want to make sure we do not miss anyone.

I will be serving as the adviser for the College Counseling majors. Since we operate as a cohort, I am going to host group advising sessions for general questions and advising on the following dates:

Tuesday, March 21: 9:30 p.m. to 10:00 p.m. EST for cohort 1
Thursday, March 23: 9:30 p.m. to 10:00 p.m. EST for cohort 2

If you would prefer to meet individually for specific questions, I am happy to work with your schedule. If you request an individual meeting, PLEASE include your name in your response below along with a few possible dates and preferred method of meeting (e.g., Blackboard Collaborate, Skype, Google Hangouts, phone, etc.). I am not concerned with the "seats" filling up for our classes, since the required courses are reserved for you, the online master's students. Therefore, rushing to register is not necessary and gaining the class schedule you need should not be an issue.

I look forward to touching base with you, hearing how you are doing, and answering any of your questions about your schedule moving forward. Thanks so much for being part of the program! As always, if you have any questions, please don't hesitate to let me know.

Have a great day and week!
Best wishes always,

Dr. Smith
[Instructor email address]

Select one response below: Are you able to attend the group advising session with your cohort?

YES Tuesday, March 21: 9:30 p.m. to 10:00 p.m. EST for cohort 1
YES Thursday, March 23: 9:30 p.m. to 10:00 p.m. EST for cohort 2

Request an individual appointment (if you select this option, please include your name and email me a few dates/times in the "General Questions" section of this chapter)

Accessibility for All Students

Every university has a different process for addressing the needs of students with varying abilities. Some campuses have a disability service office where students learn about the possible accommodations that can be made for them. When students register at the disability services office, the coordinators typically send a notification to the student's current faculty to highlight the specific accommodations for the student. Most institutions advise the faculty to then reach out to the student to discuss the accommodations moving forward. Have these conversations before the semester begins, if possible, to develop an effective plan that works for both student and instructor.

One semester I had a student who is blind in my hybrid course. The Office of Disability Services (ODS) was a wealth of information. They told me how to make my class accessible and what things to consider—but they do not actually do the work for you.

A few weeks before classes started, I got the letter informing me that my course had to be accessible for this student. I called the ODS and had a conversation about what needed to happen. The first thing they said to help ease my mind is that it does not have to be finished by the first day of classes! There are tools on the Internet, PDF converters to make sure that documents show up as text and not images, image captioning tools, voice-over tools for information that was presented, and tools that made assigned web pages accessible.

Did you know that most search engines and browsers have extensions that can be downloaded to find out the accessibility of the web page? I didn't either! But these great resources are available when needed. There are far too many types of accessibility modifications to list here; however, it is important to know that these tools exist and that the ODS (or the equivalent on your campus) is able to point you to these resources. It will, however, be your job or your TA's job to implement the accommodations.

Accessible Syllabus

Rather than simply uploading a written syllabus into the LMS, instructors can record and narrate their syllabus. Additionally, for ADA (Americans with Disabilities Act) compliance, closed captioning can be added to the syllabus to ensure that all students are able to receive the information at their own pace and time. Following the viewing of the recorded syllabus, instructors can ask a short three- to five-question quiz, which highlights questions that are important for students to know after reading the content of the syllabus. For example, one question may be a multiple-choice question like "What day and time of the week does our synchronous class meet?" or "How many times a week do we meet virtually?

Closed Captions

One semester, I applied for a captioning grant to add closed caption features to my syllabus. I used screencasting recording to narrate the contents of my syllabus. Then, a vendor reviewed my syllabus and added closed captioning to the narration. I received the file and uploaded it to the LMS. All students were appreciative of the narration and level of detail shared within the recording. As an added bonus, I didn't have to spend as much time in my synchronous class covering the details of the syllabus. I could direct students to review the syllabus and even give them specific time markers where I addressed each topic. When students had questions about a topic, I could point them to the marker where I had already covered it on the narrated syllabus.

My student evaluations through the years revealed that this addition was a success. Students with visual and auditory challenges mentioned how the narrated syllabus helped them to use their assistive devices and feel more prepared for the semester to begin.

WORD TO THE WISE: Research the ODS at your institution, keeping in mind that each office may be named something different and/or combined into another department, which often depends on the size and resources of your institution. Review the department website, the expectations of instructors for making accommodations, the process for reaching out to students or vice versa, and any other related materials. Also, check out the ADA website for learning more about the Americans with Disabilities Act (www.ada.gov).

"Let me become a sharer in life. For it is through sharing that my limitations are expanded and my gifts are utilized."—Eleesha

Resources

Anderson, L. W., & Krathwohl, D. R. (Eds). (2001). *A taxonomy for learning, teaching, and assessing: A revision of Bloom's taxonomy of educational objectives.* New York, NY: Longman.

Andrade, H. (2000). Using rubrics to promote thinking and learning. *Educational Leadership, 57*(5), 13–19. Retrieved from https://learn.vccs .edu/bbcswebdav/institution/SO/IDOL/Unit%207%20-%20Assessments/ using_rubrics.pdf

Andrade, H. (2001). The effects of instructional rubrics on student writing. *Current Issues in Education, 4*, 4. Retrieved from https://cie.asu.edu/ojs/ index.php/cieatasu/article/viewFile/1630/665

Angelo, T. A., & Patricia, C. K. (1993). *Classroom assessment techniques: A handbook for college teachers.* San Francisco, CA: Jossey-Bass.

Bloom, B. (1956). *Taxonomy of educational objectives: The classification of educational goals.* New York, NY: Longmans, Green.

Churches, A. (2008). Bloom's taxonomy blooms digitally. *Educators' eZine.* Retrieved from http://www.teachlearning.com

Dabbagh, N. (2003). Scaffolding: An important teacher competency in online learning. *TechTrends, 47*(2), 39–44. doi:10.1007/BF02763424

Goodrich, H. (1997). Understanding rubrics. *Educational Leadership, 54*(4), 14–17. Retrieved from http://www.ascd.org/publications/ educational-leadership/dec96/vol54/num04/Understanding-Rubrics.aspx

Hai-Jew, S. (2009). Scaffolding discovery learning spaces. *Journal of Online Learning and Teaching, Multimedia Educational Resource for Learning and Online Teaching.* doi:10.1007/978-1-4419-1428-6_653

Mertler, C. (2001). Designing scoring rubrics for your classroom. *Practical Assessment, Research & Evaluation, 7*(25), 1–10. Retrieved from http:// pareonline.net/getvn.asp?v=7&n=25

Moskal, B. M. (2000). Scoring rubrics: What, when, and how? *Practical Assessment, Research, & Evaluation, 7*(3). Retrieved from http://pareonline .net/getvn.asp?v=7&n=3

Mueller, J. (2016). *Authentic Assessment Toolbox: Rubrics, 2016.* Retrieved from http://jfmueller.faculty.noctrl.edu/toolbox

Nitko, A. J. (2001). *Educational assessment of students.* Upper Saddle River, NJ: Merrill.

Suthers, D., Toth, E., & Weiner, A. (1997). An integrated approach to implementing collaborative inquiry in the classroom. *Computer Supported Collaborative Learning, 97,* 10–14. Retrieved from https://scholarspace .manoa.hawaii.edu/bitstream/10125/22928/1/CSCL97.pdf

CHAPTER 9

Tips and Stories From Instructors in the Helping Professions

"Sharing is caring." That is what my doctoral teaching assistant, Courtney Walters, and I say to one another as we co-teach our online courses. We both have found significant value in sharing resources and not reinventing the wheel. This chapter encapsulates this phrase and mentality. Within the helping professions, it is essential that we continue to share and learn from each other as we navigate online education and facilitate sessions with our students.

I (Angie C. Smith) identify as an Italian-American and culturally we prepare and share food with one another to maintain community, foster relationships, and demonstrate that we care. This chapter is meant to do just that: show you that we care about you and want to provide you with tangible resources that you can use for your own teaching practice.

We are so grateful for our colleagues who shared their knowledge, content expertise, and creativity in this chapter. These contributors are colleagues in the helping vocations, and they offer tips, resources, examples, and activities for online learning. We encourage you to review the information and adapt and/or repurpose the material to fit your teaching style and students' needs. Embrace, enjoy, have fun, and pass it on!

▪ Three Ways to Engage in the Asynchronous Online Environment

Tia-Jane'l Bass

Opportunities to interact with students can be little to none when teaching a course that does not have any live or synchronous online components. For the required, online course I taught in personal health, I had to find ways for students to have an intermittent touch from me and their fellow students. The three methods that I used to interact with my students are:

- Holding virtual office hours
- Including graded discussion boards where students are required to read the comments of other students and respond substantively
- Producing voice-over PowerPoint presentations that students can watch online as videos

Virtual Office Hours

Holding virtual office hours during scheduled days of the week is the single most useful way for me to give my students access to me. These virtual office hours can be offered via a phone call, or a video call can be scheduled so that the student gets face-to-face connection with the instructor. Typically, I find that students who use the virtual office hours do not have questions about course concepts; they are mostly having trouble with some technical issue with assignment submission or they want to discuss a grade that they have earned on a particular assignment. However, in my observation, when students feel comfortable expressing themselves online, such as through an email or in a discussion board forum, they use one of those routes for asking questions before reaching out via the phone.

Graded Discussion Boards

In my asynchronous online courses, I require weekly discussion board postings. Students earn points for an original response that addresses a question about that week's subject as well as for commenting on the response of another student. I also require that these postings be substantive; the posting must be at least two complete sentences, appropriately address the core topic, and be understandable with minimal grammatical or mechanical errors. This is a great way to get students to communicate and get to know one another online, starting with the very first week's introductions.

Lectures With Voice-Over PowerPoints

Also in my asynchronous course, I use a lecture component to supplement the students' reading, videos, and other exercises. This was not required by my department, but after teaching the same course live/on-campus, I decided to do this so that students would be exposed to the information in another way and hopefully appeal to the more auditory learners. Moreover, the slides I used in my lectures contain details and examples that the students would not get in the book, just as in a live lecture. I chose a very easy method to do this: I use the record function in Microsoft PowerPoint. When students access these PowerPoints, they are able to view it like a video as the slides advance automatically with the audio. This allows students to hear my voice and perhaps even feel more connected with me as the instructor. These PowerPoints are easy to do and they are evergreen, so you can use them again and again once you have made final edits to them.

■ The Innovative Instructor

Adria S. Dunbar

I love technology, and there are a number of tools and resources that I use to help me make the most of my time and optimize the learning experience for my students. However, one day I ran into a situation where I couldn't find a good tool to help me solve a problem.

I began my career as an adjunct professor tasked with supervising students during their internship semesters. During the semester, they were required to submit weekly protected health information as an audio recording. Without a mailbox or an office, secure file sharing was a challenge. After several rounds of trying to piece together existing software, I decided to team up with a colleague and software developers to design and develop a software solution that fit the unique needs for supervisors of students completing practicum and internship field placements in the helping professions where confidentiality and privacy are a must.

I knew nothing about software development at the beginning of the project, but I knew what I liked, what I didn't like, and what I needed. I also knew a little bit about how innovation diffuses, since my dissertation focused on the topic. So I took a leap, learned a lot about software development, and worked with a team to make the tool I needed.

If you need a tool or software to fill a technology gap, then think about designing it yourself. Here are some of the lessons I learned along the way:

- Software development takes a team with experience.
- Spend all the time you need for good design on the front end.
- Step away from the project for a few days and then revisit. Step away. Revisit. This helps you see things with fresh eyes.
- Double or triple your budget. We were stuck a few times because of funding issues. Searching for funding when your software is only partially complete is not ideal.
- Broaden your user market by creating software that can be used both on web-based and mobile applications.
- Ensure compliance with the Americans with Diasabilities Act (ADA) every step of the way.
- Use project management software to keep your team on the same page.
- Beta test your software with a small group of users. There will be bugs and issues with the features. Users are really good at finding your mistakes. Let them!

The software is called Apprentice (www.apprenticesoftware).

■ Yet Another Mail Merge and Smore

Elizabeth A. Vincent

I often find myself in a situation where I need to send similar information to a group of students that also has to include information specific to the individual student. Mass emails to advisees or students can feel impersonal, and they do not add to the sense of community. So, when I found Yet Another Mail Merge (YAMM) (www.yet-another-mail-merge.com) that I could use with Google Mail and Google Sheets, I was excited to have a solution to that problem.

YAMM allows users to send emails to large groups that are both generic and have the option of providing individualized information. This tool is free for up to 400 emails a day, which also makes it affordable. It pairs with Google Sheets (part of the Google Suite), where the user creates a spreadsheet with student names, email addresses, and any specialized information I need to include in the message. I create an email and save it in my drafts folder of Google Mail, and then YAMM auto-populates the emails. It sends a test version to me first, and then sends the email to all recipients.

Here's an example:

Hello <<Name>>,

I hope your fall semester has been going well and that you are settling into your coursework at Counseling University. It is time to begin planning your courses for the spring 2018 semester, as enrollment will begin October 1, 2017. You will find my suggestions for your spring courses below.

- <<Course 1>>
- <<Course 2>>
- <<Course 3>>
- <<Additional Comments>>

If you would like to speak further about your upcoming course registration or additional advising needs, please send me an email so we can schedule a time to meet!

Best,
Your Professor

I can customize what information populates the space between the <<>>. These sections correspond with column titles within the Google Sheets spreadsheet. If you have a part-time student who is only taking two courses, and has no "Additional Comments," these two lines will disappear in that student's email message and will not create a large space or gap.

Students enjoy receiving emails like this because the email is specifically written to them individually. YAMM also saves the instructor a lot of time. It is also handy to have a spreadsheet of all advising information that you can adjust and edit over time for your own recordkeeping.

Another great feature of this tool is that it will run a live report of the recipients' use of the email. Within the Google Sheets document, it will indicate if the recipients received and opened the email. You can set a follow-up email to send if the user hasn't opened the email within a certain period of time. This ensures that information has been received, so you are able to know with certainty that the student has received your message.

Additional Uses for YAMM

I have used YAMM for managing our graduate program's admissions process to send an email to all applicants who are missing parts of their application, outlining specifically what parts are missing. I can also see using this tool to provide individual feedback on student work within a course if you are not choosing to do so within a course management system.

Smore (www.smore.com)

I use Smore to provide resources for students before class begins. Smore is an online tool that allows you to create virtual "flyers" to send to students in your class. Smore lets you create three flyers for free, but all flyers are editable on an ongoing basis, so I use the same flyer for each course every year for simplicity and cost reduction.

These are not your average flat flyers, either. Smore allows you to make live flyers with links, videos, images, forms, and other tools to make the flyer specific to your needs. In the design process, the flyer appears as a web page and is "drag and drop," so you are not wasting time on design but instead focusing on the content and information. You share your Smore flyer by sending a link to the recipients. You can then track how many people have viewed your Smore flyer to determine its impact. You can also edit the flyer in real time, allowing for ongoing changes even after you have sent out the link. I find this helpful if I locate a typo within the Smore or if a web address of a hyperlinked website has changed.

Course Introduction Using Smore

Here is how I use a Smore flyer to introduce myself and the course to my students.

- I introduce myself to students by including a picture of myself, and a brief biography, so students can get to know me to remove the mystery of who I am as a person and instructor.

- I introduce the class topic, share how I think the content is relevant to the student's professional development, and explain my own experiences with the topic.

- I outline the basics of the course: when the first class meeting will take place, a hyperlink to the academic calendar, and when the syllabus and course management web page will be available.

- I specify what technology and software are used in the course. I overview each tool and provide information and links to university web pages that describe how to get started and navigate the systems.

- I conclude with information about what to do if the technology is not working, and how to contact me with questions or help. This creates class expectations from the beginning for how to seek help, and to reduce anxieties about being penalized if the technology is not working.

Other Uses for Smore

I have used Smore as a virtual newsletter, and it could be used to communicate program-wide information to students. It could also be used for a student assignment. Often within the field of counseling, we teach students the importance of outreach and communicating with the public or collaborating organizations. Smore could be used to assist students in an outreach campaign or to share information with parents or other stakeholders related to their future professional goals.

■ Play Therapy Online and Icebreaker Turned Class Directory

Amanda Hudson Allen

Play Therapy

Last summer I was challenged with teaching a mostly hands-on experiential activity–led class in an online setting. The course was Counseling Children and Adolescents, so much of what was going to be lost in the online format was the students' opportunity to play with toys, use various expressive techniques such as art methods, and act like kids. To keep this element of the course, I found images of toys I would have brought with me to a face-to-face class. If the images are saved as individual jpeg files, they can be dragged over to the class whitespace (after content is loaded) and students can then drag and move these items at their discretion. Once the images are dragged over to the class whiteboard, you can even copy that whiteboard to the breakout rooms and students can still move the jpeg files around! This opened a floodgate of opportunities! I was able to collect jpeg figurines that my students used for "play" as they described their family dynamics in mock child/counselor sessions.

I also use jpeg files to create a play therapy room with all the toys a counselor could ever dream of! The only difference is that the images appear to move themselves instead of being moved in someone's hand as they would be in a face-to-face format.

Icebreaker Turned Class Directory

One of my new favorite icebreaker activities involves students sharing as much or as little as they'd like about themselves via Google Slides. Before starting this activity, I emphasize to the whole class the importance of each class member feeling safe. I do this to maximize the amount of information they are willing to share later on down the road and to create a classroom culture of interest in the class as people, not just names in a chat space.

I create a Google Slide (Google Slides is part of the Google suite) for each student in the class, and assign the student's name to a slide. I ask them to use a link I shared with them (with editing permissions) to find their slide, and then students are encouraged to drag and drop personal or professional related pictures to help answer the questions found on slide 2. I set a timer for 10 to 20 minutes depending on the tech savviness of the class. Once the timer has gone off, the students are asked to share their slides. They can do this by taking a screenshot of the slide and dragging it to the course whiteboard, or students can be asked to "go to slide #__ to learn more about Jane Doe." The whole class will be able to hear Jane speak through the software. The instructor can tell which slide the students are looking at because that is how Google Docs is set up.

My favorite perk of this activity in a format like Google Slides is how easy it is for students (and me) to return to this information. Once I share the Google Slides link with the class site, we have a class directory!

Useful Online Tools: Concept Mapping, Bulletin Boards, Video Assessment

Jonathan Ryan Ricks

Concept Mapping

As a method of helping students organize complex information, I have taught the use of concept maps using various free Internet websites. Students may easily build a concept map online and share with their classmates and instructor.

A concept map is a graphic organizer that helps students categorize information in manageable portions. In my counseling theories class, I assign students the task of creating an online concept map to break down the many components of a counseling framework. Afterward, I have students share the link to their map in the classroom management system (Blackboard, Moodle, etc.). I require all students to visit the gallery of created counseling theory concept maps to learn more about each theory.

I have found that this helps students master the facets of the theory more than writing discussion posts. By physically linking concepts to categories to describe a counseling theory, students come away with a greater understanding of often complicated material.

Online Bulletin Boards vs. Discussion Boards

Online bulletin boards are a great way to share information. They are free websites that allow students to add text, pictures, and videos. I often use

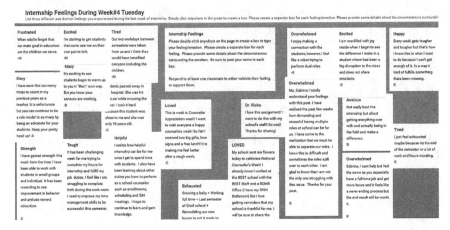

Figure 9.1 Example of an Interactive Online Bulletin Board.

online bulletin boards instead of an online discussion board. In my internship in counseling class, I ask students to post their feelings to the online bulletin board. Communicating in this format allows students to see that other students share their emotions, and it appears to be more effective than discussion board postings.

Video Assessment

I use video in assessing student work. Students enjoy this personal feedback and report that it feels like live interaction with me. In my school counseling course, students are required to create a website that demonstrates mobile applications or other technology that may help K-12 school-aged students. When providing feedback on their websites, I create a screencast using a free online program. While visiting the different pages of the student's website, I provide feedback by recording my screencast, which is simply a recording of what is viewable on my computer screen, and speak to the student as if we were meeting in person. A screenshot of this type of feedback is included here (Figure 9.1).

■ Meaningful Classroom Activities Online

Shenika Juanita Jones

The lifespan development course I teach started as a hybrid course that included both an online and a face-to-face component. However, the course is taught online-only now. While transitioning to online-only, I had to create ways of recreating meaningful classroom activities within a completely online forum. To build rapport and create a safe climate in my online classroom, I focus on quality feedback and avoid division.

Focus on Quality Feedback

The small group discussion board forums in a learning management system (LMS) are not designed to serve as group counseling sessions, but the dynamics can mirror that of a support group if students focus on the quality of feedback by acknowledging the feelings of each group member and applauding courageous actions. In courses that require students to understand their personal values and beliefs as they prepare to serve others (such as the lifespan development course), students must be encouraged to use all the elements of the technology to genuinely support their group members by providing quality replies in the online discussion forums.

Avoid Division

Like all humans, students can be creatures of habit. If students more organically connect with some group members than others, they may begin to provide replies only to those particular group members. Unintentionally, this can cause division within the discussion board forum, decrease the level of transparency, and damage rapport. To counter these potential problems, I instruct students to diversify their replies. Students are reminded to reply or collaborate with two different group members for each assignment. This expectation helps students to step outside of the box to connect with a student they would typically overlook.

Depending on the size of the group, instructors could also mandate that students reply to each of their small group members for all assignments, which could contribute to a positive and supportive learning community.

■ Creative Use of Video

Emily Erin Robinson

In any online course I teach, I send an email out about a week ahead of the scheduled start of the course to the class introducing myself and telling my students how excited I am to have them in my class. I also give them instructions for entering our Moodle site where I have posted an introductory video.

I always script my intro video because I tend to take long pauses while I think of the next thing to say, use too many filler words, and forget important things that I needed to include.

I set aside 10 to 15 minutes to film my intro video so that I have enough time to do a couple of takes if needed. In it I try to give my students a sense of who I am as a person, so I share pictures of my family, my dog, my favorite sports team, and a fun fact that most people don't know about me. I also share why I love teaching the course that they are taking. I like to keep the video between 3 and 5 minutes long because after that even I start to get bored! I also share that as the course goes on we'll get to know each other very deeply and I try to set a tone of respect for my students and their opinions. I refer to our course community and set it up as a shared group of scholars who can and will learn from one another.

I also require that my students create their own introductions, either as videos or as a discussion post with pictures attached. I require that they tell me some things about themselves as a person: hometown, family, pets, sports, hobbies, and one interesting fact. I also ask that they share what led them to take the course, and how they see the course supporting their development as a professional. Finally, I ask them to imagine that they run into me 5 years down the road in Target—what would they say about what they learned in the course then? (This also tells me who has looked at the syllabus and who hasn't.)

I try to integrate some of the information that they have shared (hometown, pets, sports team) into my discussion posts or examples. This shows that I not only care about the students as learners, but as people too. It also verifies that I actually do read their posts.

End-of-Course Student Video

Over the years I've cultivated a practice where at the end of the course, I offer my exiting students the opportunity to create a very short (no more than 30 seconds) video telling the next semester's students what they will need to do to be successful in the course, and upload it into the LMS. I splice all the videos together to make a short video that runs about 3 minutes. At the beginning of the next semester I post this video with the syllabus and encourage students to view it by having a brief quiz on it, where they have to state what their top three success strategies from the video will be. This encourages students to begin thinking about their metacognitive processes at the very beginning of the course, and it also sets the stage for us to discuss as a class the expectations that we have for our classroom community and what preparedness looks like in an online environment.

Video Paired Interview

In my co-led leadership for a diverse community course, one of our main goals is to impress upon our students that everyone has a different background and perspective, even if they look like you. To accomplish this, we do a paired interview.

In the syllabus review at the beginning of the course, I set up a poll in the LMS that offers a few dates and times that students can vote for to select a date. This is a required attendance event. All students must have a web cam or a headset with a microphone for this class.

I set up the interview spaces in rooms in Blackboard Collaborate. Students are paired and given a list of five to eight questions to choose from to ask their partner about one of their identities (female, athlete, Korean, etc.). I set 4 minutes on the stopwatch feature in the LMS so that everyone can watch the clock. For the first 2 minutes, half of the class is the interviewer and the other half is being interviewed. At the 2-minute point, I prompt the students to trade roles and begin again.

At the conclusion of the 4 minutes, I rotate half the students on to the next room and once everyone is moved, I reset the timer for 4 minutes and begin the sequence again. After they have met roughly half their classmates, I bring them back together for a large group discussion of what they learned.

Interactive Theory Education and Recreating In Vivo Role-Play Online

Nicole Childs

In vivo role-play gives students the opportunity to practice and apply theory and techniques in counseling as if they were actual counselors. While this type of experience can be easily created in a face-to-face setting, barriers exist for the online setting.

For my online students enrolled in a theories and techniques in counseling course, I used synchronous and asynchronous online resources and services. This was built on movie presentation analysis and Google Doc spreadsheet.

Movie Presentation Analysis

This is a good tool for asynchronous courses. Each student selects a movie character from a movie chosen by the instructor. When the instructor provides the movie, every student has to watch it and is aware of the character development within the film. Try to select a movie that is free for students to watch. In groups of two, students are expected to analyze the development of a character using one theory of therapy. Students should provide the following information: a brief overview of selected counseling theory, an explanation of movie character dysfunction or behavior, a counseling plan and goals for this character, the role/stance of the counselor, therapy techniques, and role-play of techniques. For the role-play, students can use YouTube video clips of their role-plays and PowerPoints using the audio caption. This student presentation can be uploaded into the week's required material and viewed by other students in the class. That way, students have online access to theoretical knowledge and application for each theory discussed in class.

Interactive Google Doc Spreadsheet

The innate interactivity of Google Docs and Google Spreadsheets makes them very useful for online educators. This is helpful in both asynchronous and synchronous courses. One way I use them is to provide a framework of the theories discussed in class and then have students fill out the blanks in an interactive Google Spreadsheet. The instructor can edit student assertions. The ultimate result is a brilliant depiction of all of the theories addressed during the course that not only serves as a resource for the final exam, but also benefits students in the future when they prepare for licensure examination.

▪ Code of Ethics and Confidentiality Statement

Shanita Brown

Building a sense of community in the classroom requires student collaboration, open dialogue, and being authentic and transparent in my expectations as an instructor. By creating a student-centered safe atmosphere, students become more accountable for their contributions and I am more accountable to the selected teaching strategies.

The purpose of a Code of Ethics or Confidentiality Agreement is to establish a safe, positive online environment for students to share personal information for rich class discussions and student learning. For example, in a multicultural lifespan development course, students dialogue on discussion boards and live sessions on topics about their adolescence, and it is vital to keep this information private and confidential.

The Code of Ethics or Confidentiality Agreement serves three purposes:

1. To enforce ethical responsibility for students to maintain privacy and respect of all information shared on discussion boards and live sessions.

2. To validate my teaching philosophy of demonstrating a caring attitude.

3. To create a safe, positive environment to facilitate student learning and growth.

It is critical to explain the rationale for the ethics statement on the first day of class, as it assists with creating a warm foundation for the course. All students must post their full name to affirm the statement before they can engage in any discussion boards or live sessions.

The instructor may also collaborate with students during the first week of class for ideas and assistance in creating the agreement. This can be done with a survey or poll. It is a good idea to include examples of acceptable and unacceptable behavior statements for the learning community. For example, "our primary goal is to learn from each other," "respect others' rights to hold different values and beliefs," "criticize the statement, not the person," and "do not reference class discussions on social media."

The following is a generic agreement that you can use as is or adjust so that it fits.

Code of Ethics/Confidentiality Agreement

As a student enrolled in _____ at [university/college name], I understand that due to the personal information that will be shared on the discussion boards and live sessions, it is VERY important that I uphold the ethical and confidentiality responsibility regarding personal information discussed. I, the undersigned, reviewed and understand the following statements:

• All information discussed online is confidential, and should not be used for purposes other than its intended use for reflection board and class. (What is discussed in class stays in class.)

- I have an ethical responsibility to maintain the privacy of all students in this class.

- Unauthorized use of confidential information will result in an "F" grade, and also be taken up with the University's Office of Student Code of Conduct.

*Print Name:*_____ *Student ID #*_____
*Date:*_____

Please post that you have read this Code of Ethics/Confidentiality Agreement and will abide by it and maintain the privacy of all students in class

■ Role-Play Activity for Synchronous and Asynchronous Courses

Courtney B. Walters

I have used variations of this activity in group supervision and internship class settings in online courses. Students seem to be more comfortable participating in role-plays when a story is provided, so I develop a few client scenarios that reflect our case discussions to provide opportunities to process particular issues or diagnoses. Each scenario provides a client description, and also instructs the "client" to keep a secret or continue a particular behavior until the "helping professional" does or asks something specific.

This activity is easily adapted to my synchronous courses by using web conferencing (e.g., Blackboard Collaborate, WebEx). The scenarios are randomly assigned and emailed to the students prior to class or sent via private messages during class. Students role-play the scenarios during class using video and/or audio.

I also modify this activity for my asynchronous courses. After randomly assigning the client scenarios, students are paired and upload to a discussion forum the video or audio recordings of their role-plays. The instructor and other students will provide written feedback in the forum after viewing/listening to recordings.

■ Our Online Slumber Party: Practicum Group Supervision

Helen Shulman Lupton-Smith

The notion of a slumber party theme ran through my first online practicum. I served as the supervisor and had three female online school counseling supervisees. Our section used VSee as the secure online technology for group sessions, which enabled us to see everyone simultaneously on the computer screen. We met weekly every Monday night from 8:00 p.m. to 9:30 p.m. This online forum was a uniquely connecting experience for all of us.

The students and I referred to our Monday class as our slumber party, because, since it was an evening class, everyone was in a winding-down mode and at home after a long day. The students wore more relaxed home clothes like sweatshirts, sweatpants, and so forth. We laughed at how the students would put their hair up in buns for class as a way of "letting their hair down." Cats and dogs could be seen running through the screen occasionally, and every now and then a child might pop up to say good night. These personal touches were part of the group supervision moments that gave all of us a window into each other's lives that would not have happened in a typical classroom setting.

There is something comforting and intimate about learning in your own home while still being able to see who you are working with. Also, having all students in the class from the same concentration of school counseling really heightened the modeling and learning that went on. From a supervisor perspective, the relaxed tone of the group enhanced learning and helped provide a trusting forum for students to process practicum anxiety. Simply referring to our group as our Monday night slumber party gives a glimpse of our group tone which was one of humor, relaxed connection, with some metaphor used throughout.

Techniques for Connecting

We used four activities in the practicum group supervision that stood out to me as promoting connection and learning

1. Build Rapport: Around the beginning of the semester, all supervisees and I took the online strengths survey called the VIA (Values in Action). VIA gives immediate feedback of one's strengths profile. One's top five strengths are called the signature strengths which are instrumental to how one operates in the world. The lower strength areas out of a total 24 are areas to be considered for further development. We had to guess the signature strengths of each other in a group and then individually talked and reflected about our profiles.

2. Grow Skills Together: In the practicum, it is important for skill development and technique development for all of us to see the sessions and techniques that were used with clients. All counseling videos were shared in secure folders on Google Drive. Students were asked to share in everyone's Google Drive folder their case conceptualization video or a counseling strategy used for their toolbox assignment. We would then take a time break and everyone would go watch the video on their own computer and come back with the group to process.

3. Midterm Feedback: During midterm, supervisees were asked to provide intentional, holistic verbal feedback to each other during group supervision. They were also asked to provide a metaphor of where each person was in the process. Both activities built on the cohesion we were developing as a group.

4. Wrapping Up. At the end of the semester, we each drew two pictures of ourselves side by side: one representing each person at the beginning of the practicum semester and one at the end. As each person discussed her own

picture, the ultimate theme of the activity was that we had all grown and taken something positive from each other which contributed to that growth.

▪ The STEPs to Taking Progress Notes

Rhonda Sutton

Most of us who become counselors do so because we want to listen, to help others, and to guide people through challenging situations and difficult experiences. Our goal, as counselors, is to be there *with* the client and *for* the client. However, it is the written documentation—the progress notes we take—that informs and guides our work as professionals.

An organized, efficient, and streamlined method for taking progress notes helps us be more effective counselors. I like to use the STEPs method for taking progress notes.

The "S" stands for subject(s) and symptoms. *Subjects* refers to the topics your client discusses, such as relationship problems, drug use, career concerns, and infertility. The symptoms are either disclosed by the client or observed by the counselor, and these can be documented in terms of emotional symptoms (anger, depression), behavioral symptoms (agitation, lethargy), cognitive symptoms (racing thoughts, memory problems), and physical symptoms (headache, nausea).

The "T" in STEPs refers to therapeutic tools. This part of the note refers to the work you did with the client, indicating both the therapeutic approaches undertaken as well as action verbs indicating the techniques you, as the counselor, used to guide, assist, and support the client during the session. It is also helpful to document the type of therapy approach used (i.e., cognitive behavioral, existential, narrative). You also need to use action verbs (aligned, demonstrated, explored, summarized) to begin sentences that reflect the tools and interventions undertaken with the client during the session.

The "E" refers to evaluation of the client's functioning and progress. Use a scale of 1 to 10, with 1 indicating that the client is not in a state ready for therapy to 10 meaning that the client has met goals and is ready to be discharged. What number would you assign your client and why? In terms of your client's progress, questions to consider include: Was the client engaged in therapy? Is the client resistant, withdrawn, stuck? It is important for your progress note to indicate some form of evaluation regarding both how well your client is doing overall and how well your client is improving within therapy.

"P" denotes the plan. This part of the progress note focuses on the short- and long-term goals for the client. The action items the client agreed to undertake between sessions are documented in this STEP. Sentences in this section, such as "the client will develop, explore, identify," and so forth, help you document the work the client will undertake to meet goals. It is important to review this section before the next session so that you can check in with the client about homework assigned and review progress toward goals.

These STEPs outline the STEPnotes method for taking progress notes. The STEPnotes format is available online, and further information can be found in my book, *The Counselor's STEPs for Progress Notes: A Guide to Clinical Language and Documentation.* There are STEPnotes formats for mental health as well as school and career counselors, and these formats are available through the online system. The book provides comprehensive information about progress notes, from how to write them, to how to store them, and what to do when someone requests them.

Given my experience as both a licensed counselor and supervisor of counselors in training, I created STEPnotes with the goal of helping counselors be more efficient, more effective, and more confident with their documentation and progress notes.

■ Distance Teaching Ideas

Elizabeth Grady

Book clubs or small-group guided discussions are used to engage students, create community, foster engagement and cooperation, and limit the isolation that is sometimes reported by distance learning students.

In think-aloud sessions, I ask students to work through problems online together in small groups or with the whole class synchronously. I give each student a few minutes to brainstorm ideas and then make a short presentation.

I ask students to create concept maps to show relationships between concepts or ideas. Students can use a variety of free software to create the maps. They upload their maps to the course site so all can comment or provide feedback, rate each one, or vote for their favorite.

Cooperative Learning: Assign students to small groups or pairs and ask them to complete topics using video conferencing or chat spaces. Have students present ideas to the whole class via slides or documents that can be uploaded and shared to forum or chat spaces.

If students are local, I assign them to groups or pairs and have them take field trips to locations that will add to their experiential learning. I ask students to take pictures or videos and create multimedia presentations to be uploaded for the whole class to review.

I ask students to demonstrate or practice skills via video, and then present clips to the whole class by uploading the content of their presentation. Allow other students to provide feedback or comments on each video to encourage engagement and collaboration.

I let my students be a panel of experts. I ask students to study a specific aspect of a theory or practice area and act as the expert in presenting the ideas to the rest of the class. Presentations are 5-minute-long video clips to demonstrate understanding of the course content.

I arrange guest speakers and facilitate their presentation online so that the class can watch the presentation live (like a live webinar) and respond to the material being presented in real time by asking questions and making comments.

In addition to live lectures, I record pieces of lecture so that the content can be viewed synchronously or asynchronously by students. Other forms of multimedia can also be used to present content, such as pictures, videos, slideshows, cognitive maps, graphic designs, and other visual representations of content.

I ask students to create role-play scenarios to be used in class or create scenarios ahead of time and ask students to act out the roles synchronously, while observers provide comments and feedback online. This can be done live, or recorded and presented at a later time.

I use simulation when practice of skills is necessary for successful course completion. Ask students to simulate counseling sessions and record and upload clips. Students can critique their own videos first, and then peers can comment and provide feedback on areas of strengths and weaknesses. I use simulation in conjunction with theoretical frameworks or skill-based approaches.

Service Learning Online

Kimberly Allen

I teach in the Youth, Family, and Community Science program, and with few exceptions, my students come into class with a goal to improve the world by supporting youth and families. We serve nontraditional distance education students, and their passion is evident in the work they are doing in their community. Knowing that my students come to class with existing skills and practical life experiences, I work to engage with my students in real-life applied social science assignments, also called *service learning*. I incorporate service learning in every class I teach. In my family life coaching courses, students practice coaching skills with volunteer clients. In my youth development course, students work in teams to create online educational tools on a topic of their choice, and then promote that tool via social media. In the parenting and family life education course, students engage in three service learning applied projects as a scaffolding approach to learning.

When students come to a parenting and family life education class, they need to know not only theory, but also the practical elements of program development, such as evidence-based practices, needs assessments, and community engagement. In order for my students to learn by doing, they complete three applied assignments: an educational plan for a family-identified need, creation of a video to explain a parenting concept, and implementation of an evidence-based curriculum training to a group of parents. To ease into the process of working with families, students begin by collecting a needs assessment from one family. They interview parents and identify their strengths and areas of concern and then they research parenting programs and resources on the identified topics. Students create an educational plan to help inform parents of possible strategies to improve the concerns or further strengthen their family. Based on the information they find in their research, students are then required to complete a 2- to 4-minute educational video highlighting those strategies. Because so many families now gather their family life information online, this is an opportunity for students to become comfortable with online educational formatting. Finally, the students further research community needs, and then develop and implement a family life or parenting educational workshop to a group in their community. With each assignment, students must submit an academic reflection paper as well as verbally process the results of each activity in a full class setting.

All three of these activities honor students' interests and ability to connect with real families in their community. Although our course readings and lectures cover the foundational information, theory, and program planning, there is no substitute for actually having students apply their knowledge in real life. Having tried this several times, here are my tips for successfully completing an applied social sciences assignment.

1. **Clear instructions and expectations are critical**. Applied work might very well be a new concept, so clarity really helps.

2. **Students guide the process**; they select and do the work themselves. Once the project is launched, much of what happens is outside of your control.

3. **Promote meaningful experiences**.

4. **Be available to answer questions** as they arise. And they will; students will want to get your opinion about everything from the topic to the process.

5. **Offer resources and tips to students.** If technology is a part of the assignment, be sure to offer resources to help the student know how to navigate the technology. There are plenty of tutorials on most technology, and steering students to good resources helps them to be successful.

6. **Give students time to process their results**. Talking about and sharing stories of applied assignments is the final step for helping students synthesize what they learn. That way students can learn from each other's experiences and have a chance to process lessons learned.

7. **Celebrate success**. Completing a service learning project is an accomplishment, and taking time to celebrate and share those successes is important. I share mine via kudos on social media—a great way to support students and bring attention to their important work.

Regardless of the specifics, students tell me that they love making a real contribution in their community, and they value applied learning. Service learning is a chance for our students to create impact and do a small part to improve the world by supporting youth and families for academic credit.

For more information, check out the following resource:

Resources

Seifer, S. D., & Connors, K. (2007). Faculty toolkit for service learning in higher education. Vanderbilt University. Retrieved from: https://www.vanderbilt.edu/oacs/wp-content/uploads/sites/140/faculty-toolkit-for-service-learning.pdf

◾ Online Resources for the Helping Professional

Kerri Brown-Parker

Many web-based tools and apps are useful for facilitating conversations, coming to consensus, providing resources to clients/students, and more. These online resources can be used in multiple ways by professionals looking to connect to others in a contemporary way. The tools are broken down into categories and charts fitting the needs of the many different roles that helping professionals fill for clients, students, and so forth. Some tools can certainly be used in more than one "category" of professional responsibility. At the time of printing, the tools included in the charts were free, although some have advanced features that require payment of a fee. These tools were included with a "liberal" belief system about privacy; please check privacy policies and terms of use to determine if they are appropriate for your needs.

NOTE: Due to the ever-changing nature of web-based tools, it is possible that these tools will be unavailable after the publishing date of this *book;* consider trying the "wayback machine" to see what the tool looked like if it is no longer available.

TEACHING TOOLS → To provide or assist in courses, workshops, skill development, personality development, technology skill development, and informational support

Online Instruction Tools/Lessons/etc.:	Survey/Quizzing Tools:	Interactive Video, Games and Text Tools:
Blendspace Explain Everything Educreations VoiceThread Weebly Screencastify Screencast-O-Matic	Google Forms Kahoot Quizziz	PlayPosit YouTube Playlist EdPuzzle Actively Learn TinyTap VideoNotes

METHODS TO SHARE RESOURCES → Helping clients/students through resource guides, awareness of opportunities, research, occupational exploration, informational support, information gathering, and so forth.

Save/Collect and Share Resources:	Create Quick Websites/ Online Information Portals:	Create Print Information Guides:
Symbaloo PearlTrees LiveBinders Diigo	Smore Weebly Tackk Wix Google Sites	Canva

CLIENT EXPRESSION → Technology tools to help students express identity, needs, and so forth through online creations. Useful in self-efficacy, self-concept, emotional support, assessment reflection/support, identifying life themes, and so forth.

Clients Create a Movie or Animated Slideshow:	Comic Creators:	Image Editors/Creators:
iMovie Animoto Adobe Spark (and Adobe Spark Page) VoiceThread WeVideo	Pixton StoryboardThat PhotoComic Make Beliefs	ThingLink Pic Collage PicMonkey Tellagami Voki Pixlr

REFLECTION → These tools can be helpful in creating reflection activities, interpreting tests, giving informational support, creating goals, making plans, and so forth.

Documents/Infographic Creators:	Create a Mind Map/ Graphic Organizer/ Plan:	Come to Agreement/"Vote" on Decisions:
Canva Google Docs Easely Piktochart	Popplet Lucidcharts Mindmeister StoryboardThat Google Draw	Dotstorming Tricider Loomio

EMOTIONAL SUPPORT → Tools for building relationships with clients, communicating outside of in-person meetings, providing emotional support or "checking in."

Text, Phone/Voicemail, Video Calling:	Online Board to Post Thoughts:	Social Media:
Remind Bloomz Google Voice Google Hangouts	Padlet Linoit	Twitter Facebook Instagram

REFLECTIVE QUESTIONS

1. After reviewing the activities, tips, and strategies, what activity could you use or adapt for your own course?

2. What concrete steps will you take to incorporate and implement the activity or tip into your course?

3. What activity meets a learning objective for your course?

4. What resources are available for your content area to build engagement and community in your course?

CHAPTER 10

What NOT to Do: Mistakes, Glitches, and Lessons Learned the Hard Way

VIGNETTE

As instructors, there are times when we wish could turn back the clock and change the way we approached an assignment, an interaction with a student, or perhaps how we designed an entire course or semester. We all could share lessons from the field and words of hope to help each other as we learn from our mistakes and awkward experiences.

As we reflect on our experiences, it's important to be gentle with ourselves and remember that we are all imperfect beings who are on a quest of continuous learning. I am inspired by a quote from Og Mandino: "Whenever you make a mistake or get knocked down by life, don't look back at it too long. Mistakes are life's way of teaching you."[1]

As a novice online instructor, I wanted to transition all my on-campus course content into my new online course. However, I did not anticipate all the adaptations and options. As the saying goes, "sometimes you don't know what you don't know." I assumed that I could engage with my students *just like* I did in the on-campus courses. However, I did not have the luxury of seeing their expressions and nonverbal communication. I soon learned that in the synchronous (i.e., Blackboard Collaborate) environment, I had to get creative . . . and quickly! I started slowly, but I swiftly learned to use polling features to test the "pulse" of my students periodically and break down my activities into smaller parts to create opportunities for built-in engagement and interaction.

---

[1]positivemotivation.net

As I polled my students about the content, it helped me get a grasp on where they were at in this moment. The polling questions helped me gauge how well (or not) the students received the material. I then asked follow-up questions and offered points of clarification, as needed.

REFLECTIVE QUESTIONS

1. Think back about a course you have taught on-campus. Can you remember an example of a time you wish you could go back and change something you did or said? What can you learn from this experience?

2. Imagine you are at the end of your course and reading your course evaluations. What are three comments you hope to read from your students?

3. What mistakes do you fear that you will make while teaching in a fully online, blended, and/or hybrid format course? What two to three concrete steps can you take to avoid and/or eliminate these fears?

4. How can you incorporate engagement and interaction into your online course? How can you reframe your content to elicit connection and communication among your students?

Mistakes, Glitches, and Lesson Learned

Mistakes, missteps, glitches, and interruptions are going to happen. We've made them, and you will too! So will your students. Some of these mishaps make the best stories and fondest memories. The key is to learn the lesson by remembering, reflecting, and adapting.

Here are some of the important (and silly) mistakes we've made and the lessons we learned. We hope you can learn from our experiences and errors.

Lesson Learned: Say Exactly What You Mean

After teaching online for more than 10 years, it finally happened. I conducted a synchronous session and only one student attended. It wasn't completely by accident, but it was unexpected.

I hosted a discussion session for students who wanted additional information about an upcoming assignment. Although my classes are asynchronous, I offer voluntary opportunities for students to ask questions in real time. So I poll students to find a convenient time for the students who would like to discuss the assignment in real time. Students who don't participate are not penalized and the session is even recorded. I am also transparent and tell students that it's helpful for me to have someone to talk to instead of simply making a recording of the instructions or anticipating questions. I said verbatim, "If at least one student shows up, it's helpful." Well, they took me seriously. One student showed up. I am sure they did not collude to make that happen, but I had to be prepared to move forward with that one student. Having only one person attend was a little bit of a blow to my ego! But it was still an effective session and the student received some personal attention.

In the end, she turned in one of the best submissions in the class.

Takeaway: Say exactly what you mean and be explicit with expectations. I also learned that offering a grade of any kind (yes/no on participation even works) effectively motivates students to participate.

Lesson Learned: Set Personal Time Boundaries

I taught my first online course a few weeks after I graduated from my doctoral program. As a new instructor, I was really excited, and my perfectionist tendencies to create the most engaging experience for my students came pouring out. I had this idea that if I didn't respond to every single discussion forum post, students would think that I was not doing my job and that I was not engaged or present. I was spending between 10 and 20 hours per week responding in length to each student's comments. By spring break, I was feeling burned out.

I shared with the students how I was feeling about the semester up to this point. In the Blackboard Collaborate meeting (i.e., synchronous), I announced that I was going to be posting a bit less in the coming weeks. There is a "hand clap" button in Blackboard Collaborate and all the students began "clapping their hands" and sharing how they were so happy that I was going to take a bit of a break. Some students even commented in the chat box that they couldn't even keep up with responding to the two to three response posts they were required to complete each week, let alone respond to every post in Moodle. Lesson learned! We all had a great laugh together about it!

Lesson Learned: Technology 101

Do not make assumptions about the technology use and skill levels of your online students. As adult learners enter our classroom space, they bring varying experiences and comfort levels with technology. Using the first class to review the technology and offer students the opportunity to practice or play with the features in the learning management system (LMS) is extremely helpful and can reduce anxiety and the unknown.

Friendly tips: During the first synchronous class in the semester, focus on two goals:

1. Build rapport and get familiar with one another.
2. Practice technology and invite students to engage in the space with the hope of becoming more comfortable in the online environment.

Lesson Learned: Organize and Automate

I really work hard at being organized and on time. I really do, especially when teaching, whether in a face-to-face class or online. However, I still often struggle with time management, specifically with arriving on time. I never seem to allow enough time, so I leave just in the nick of time, and often need to rush to get to where I am going on time.

Teaching my first online course many years ago was an eye-opener in this regard. I left my office on campus with plans of arriving home just in time to provide students access to their final exam. It would have worked out perfectly had it not been for the traffic jam I encountered on my route home. In an attempt to problem-solve, I drove into a McDonald's parking lot and tried to connect my laptop to the free Wi-Fi so that I could provide access to the test and my problem would be solved. Right? Unfortunately, after 5 minutes of trying to connect, I was unsuccessful. I ran inside with my laptop and set up shop at one of the tables. Still no luck connecting to the Wi-Fi. I ran to the counter for help, only to have to wait. Finally, I was able to ask the cashier about the Wi-Fi. She indicated that the modem had been offline for days now. By this time, students should have already had access to the exam. I started to receive a few emails from my students wondering where the exam was. I also received a few phone calls and a voicemail. Frantically, I rushed out of the restaurant's door and back to my car. I drove around looking for another Wi-Fi option. I finally found a Dunkin Donuts with Wi-Fi that worked. I was able to click the appropriate button on Blackboard, giving students access to the exam. Though it seemed like forever, the exam was released only 8 minutes late, according to my watch.

Takeaway: Online education always takes more time that you think it will. Also, take advantage of all the bells and whistles the LMS offers. In advance, set dates and times for modules and exams to be released automatically. And if you are in need of Wi-Fi, look for a Dunkin Donuts!

Lesson Learned: Expect the Unexpected

I was attending my synchronous class from a hotel room at a conference in Florida. With about 15 minutes remaining in the class, the hotel fire alarm went off. My students began asking if I was OK and expressed sincere concern for my safety. I used this opportunity to demonstrate crisis management skills. I calmly shared that I was fine but needed to leave the building due to the alarm. I asked my teaching assistant to take over the final 10 minutes of class and shared with the students that I would email them later to let them know I was OK. I quickly exited the building with my laptop and made it out of the building safely. I had several emails waiting in my inbox from students asking if I made it out of the building. What a way to build rapport with my students!

Takeaway: Expect the unexpected! Prepare students in advance whenever possible, but when the unexpected occurs, roll with it and remain calm. It's all going to be OK!

Lesson Learned: The Unresponsive Student

In one of my first courses teaching online, one of my students attended the first three Blackboard Collaborate sessions and appeared to be actively engaged in our Moodle online community. About the fourth week of class, I noticed that she was not attending the required weekly Blackboard Collaborate meetings and was not posting contributions to the discussion forums. My teaching assistant and I reached out to her several times throughout the week with no response. Several weeks passed and we were getting increasingly concerned that we were not hearing back from her. I ended up calling her and leaving her a few messages. After several attempts and toward the end of the semester, she emailed me back and shared a tragic event that had occurred in her life. She was distraught, struggling, grieving, and unable to connect to the class due to the personal loss.

You will undoubtedly run across a student who is unresponsive. Students are unresponsive for various reasons, which may not be related to their lack of interest in the course.

TAKEAWAYS

1. On the syllabus, stress the importance of communication and sharing. Then, highlight the rationale as to why this is so important in an online class. I now share this story or some version of it in my online courses to demonstrate how it can affect the student's grade and future with the program.

2. On the syllabus, in Moodle, or verbally in a synchronous session, include specific examples of concrete expectations and explicitly state the number of calendar days in which you will and/or will not accept an assignment (i.e., 5 calendar days after the due date with the percentage, grade, and/or point deduction included) and highlight the institution's policy concerning absences, missed classes, and so forth.

Lesson Learned: Engaging the Passive Student

Inevitably, in every synchronous session I teach, one student is not interested in actively participating and engaging in the session. If a student doesn't respond to polls, I privately chat with the student to check in to see if everything is OK. If I do not hear from them, especially repeat offenders, I may call on them by name in the public chat box.

Takeaway: Develop a plan for how you will engage and invite passive students to participate. Just as in the face-to-face classroom, not everyone is going to be willing to participate all the time. We have all types of learners in our space.

Lesson Learned: Require Students to Use the University Email Address

Students may have multiple email addresses from accounts as a student, employee, personal/home, and so forth. In the beginning of the semester, indicate that you will be corresponding with them using their official university email address only. In the past, I have had students use their personal email addresses and then tell me that they did not receive my correspondence about assignments and request more time to complete them. This is very difficult to prove, so set this expectation up front.

Also, through the years we have seen some very creative email addresses, and we prefer not to correspond with "QuietEssence," "FoxyMama32," or "HillTopBBaller," although it is pretty entertaining to associate the owners with the email addresses.

Takeaway: In the syllabus, indicate your preferred method of communication and require students to use their university email address. Most universities have a system where students can link their personal and university email accounts together. Therefore, when the sender emails the student at either account, the email will be delivered and merged within this one portal. Students should be able to view all emails from both email accounts.

Lesson Learned: Expect Interruptions

One semester, I was teaching a synchronous course from my home office when my 7-year-old daughter ran down the stairs and proceeded to vomit all over the floor outside my home office door. My partner gave me the "thumbs up" that he had it covered and she would be OK. However, in these types of situations, there can be conflicts of interest. As the instructor, do you run to your child or do you maintain the structure and continuity of the classroom experience while in panic mode? (By the way, she was fine and recovered quickly.)

Takeaway: Expect and prepare for interruptions. If you or your students have family and pets, it is a good idea to have a partner or babysitter available to support you while you are hosting your synchronous session. Usually, synchronous sessions last for no more than 2 hours.

Lesson Learned: Return the Right Paper to the Right Student

In my first semester of teaching, I had two students with the same last name and first initial, which created some obvious confusion, and I accidentally mixed up their papers and returned the wrong paper to the wrong student. Luckily, the paper was not too personal and I quickly retracted it.

Takeaway: All instructors are apt to return a paper to the wrong student at least once in their career. Check, double-check, and check again the names of students before returning assignments. Also, in the syllabus, request that students save their documents using their first and last name as well as the course number or assignment. For example, Angie.Smith. CAREERPAPER.doc

Consistency and specificity can be very helpful in avoiding these types of errors.

Lesson Learned: Sometimes Pets Join the Class

I strive to offer an inclusive classroom where everyone and every "body" is welcome. On several occasions, we have been in our synchronous space and, out of nowhere, a series of random letters pops up in one student's chat box. I chat back to the student with a question mark, seeking an explanation. The student explained that her cat walked across the computer keys and thus joined us in the session. Sometimes students will show their pets on the camera, which can also create a warm, welcoming environment.

Takeaway: In the beginning of the semester, share with students the inclusive nature of your class. Share examples of when things like this may have occurred in the past, and if it happens to them they should simply let you know. Everyone has a laugh about it and enjoys the humor!

Lesson Learned: The Instructor Sees All

In my first year of teaching, there were two students who were discussing in a private chat message their disinterest in the course content. I privately messaged them both to remind them that instructors could see all of their communication in the synchronous space, including private chats. I asked them to remain after the synchronous session to discuss further. The students were surprised and very apologetic.

Takeaway: In the beginning of the semester, be sure to let students know that you are able to view all comments made in the synchronous space. Beware and be aware of all content shared in "private" chats and other online modalities.

Lessons Learned: Release Assignments and Exams When You Say You Will

Students can't begin the exam or an assignment if you have not given them access to it.

I once created a two-part exam. Part 1 was submitted via upload before the final exam. The second part of the exam was a timed, open-book, true/false, multiple-choice exam that I thought I had scheduled to open automatically at 11:30 a.m. However, I mistakenly scheduled it to open at 11:30 p.m. Imagine the email fury from the students when they could not open the exam at 11:30 a.m.! We came to the mutual decision to use the uploaded information as the final assignment.

Depending on the university, the LMS may automatically open the course and learning modules on the first day of the semester and on scheduled class days, or instructors may have to initiate opening the content to the students. Find out the process for your institution before the first day of class. Either way, in the pre-semester welcome letter, communicate with students when the course will be opened to them and in the syllabus state explicitly on what days new content will be open.

TAKEAWAYS

1. As you create assignments, be sure to add calendar reminders to your schedule or calendar as reminders to open content on the specified time and date.

2. If possible, in your LMS, check out the "student view" after making changes on your screen to verify that the changes you made are indeed showing up on the student portal as well.

3. Be flexible and understand that the best plans can be interrupted by user error! When possible, collaborate with students to come to a solution when mistakes happen.

Top 15 Things NOT to Do When Teaching in the Online Learning Environment

1. Start planning a day before the semester begins.
2. Join a synchronous session in a public venue.
3. Assume that students know the expectations and logistics of the course.
4. Forget to test the technology you plan to use for the course.
5. Do it alone.
6. Remain silent or undercommunicate.
7. Wait until the final day that grades are due to grade all assignments.
8. Indicate that you are going to open a learning module/content on a specific day, then neglect to open it.
9. Forget to delete previous student information and/or dates when you copy over content from one semester to another.
10. Create a discussion forum in a student learning center, then forget to respond to the student questions throughout the semester. (Friendly tip: To remedy this issue, you can set the forum questions from students in your LMS to go directly to your email.)
11. Forget about accessibility of the course for all students.
12. Consider pedagogy as secondary to technology.
13. Think that there cannot be a sense of community in an online environment.
14. Forget personal touches and small details. Students appreciate when you send them a personal email and remember important information about what they shared in class.
15. Neglect to celebrate milestones. Throughout the semester, students have gotten married, had babies, children graduated, and other amazing opportunities to celebrate big milestones in their lives. Take the time to celebrate with them when appropriate. For example, when one student in our class had her baby girl, I created a virtual card in a synchronous

space and all students shared words of encouragement and signed it. I sent the card to the student and uploaded it to our LMS for everyone to be able to view.

▪ Guided Reflections

Let's personalize your "what not to do" list. As you consider teaching in the online environment, list five potential pitfalls that may cause your course to derail. (*For example, plan ahead for your own self-care and develop a plan to grab a glass of water before you start, collect all materials for your synchronous "live" session, silence your phone, and DO NOT forget to use the restroom before class begins.*)

HELPFUL TIP: When teaching online, self-care is so important to consider. Make sure your battery and body are fully charged when teaching your class, or else you will suddenly leave the space and your students stranded without their instructor—both physically and mentally.

"Experience is simply the name we give our mistakes."—Oscar Wilde

CHAPTER 11

Ethical Considerations for Online Instruction in the Helping Professions

University instructors largely are responsible for the development and delivery of instruction. Great efforts are often taken to ensure that instruction satisfies curriculum requirements and promotes student learning. Less thought, however, may be given to other elements of instruction, such as the potential for ethical violations or academic dishonesty.

Regardless of the mode of instruction, ethical considerations should be interwoven in all facets of teaching and instructional delivery. This is especially the case for instructors who teach in online learning environments. Given the continuous evolution of online learning, careful attention must be paid to the ways in which instruction is adapted, developed, and delivered. In some instances, the potential for ethical violation is so subtle that it may not be readily obvious. As one might imagine, the risk for ethical dilemmas and breach of ethical practice in online learning environments is more prevalent than ever before.

This chapter provides an overview of the intersection of academic integrity and professional ethics in online instruction. Both instructors and students maintain responsibility for demonstrating ethical behaviors. Therefore, this chapter outlines ethical considerations for both parties within the contexts of education and the helping professions. A case example is provided to demonstrate the online instructor's role in promoting academic integrity and professionally ethical behavior. Finally, resources are provided to support instructors' efforts to deliver sound instruction and navigate ethical dilemmas should they arise.

OVERARCHING QUESTIONS

What comes to mind when you think of academic integrity?

Does your profession's code of ethics include language related to online learning?

_____

How have you, a colleague, or former instructor addressed academic integrity or professional ethics in coursework?

_____

VIGNETTE

An online instructor teaching a group counseling course requires students to participate in mock group counseling sessions during the synchronous portions of the course. Personal growth and self-awareness are expected outcomes of the mock sessions. The instructor encourages students to share about their life experiences during the exercise, but warns them to use caution when sharing sensitive information because confidentiality cannot be guaranteed. The instructor asks all students to use headsets and participate in the sessions from a secure confidential location. He then learns from a student that another student enrolled in the group course has allowed several of her friends to listen in on the mock sessions. Although the syllabus does not explicitly state that this is not allowed, the instructor has implied that sharing student information gleaned from the mock sessions is inappropriate.

1. Is the sharing student behaving in an unethical manner? If so, how?

   _____

   _____

2. Should the instructor confront the student whom she believes is allowing friends to listen to the sessions?

   _____

   _____

3. What are potential repercussions of this student's behavior, if you believe it to be unethical?

   _____

   _____

4. What strategies can the instructor use to attempt to prevent situations like this from occurring in the future?

   _____

   _____

■ Codes of Ethics for Instructors

In general, ethics are moral principles that guide behavior. A helping professional whose decisions are driven by the use of a moral compass as a guiding light will be keenly aware of the manner in which ethics impacts the delivery of online instruction. In these instances, students often experience the benefit of an instructor who demonstrates the following principles: autonomy, nonmaleficence, beneficence, and justice, among others.

Instructors who are principled in autonomy appreciate independence and self-direction. They allow students the opportunity to grow and develop with guided support, learning from successes and their mistakes along the way. It is critical for instructors to contribute to the growth and development of the students they teach; beneficence is at the core of what instructors do. On the other side of this coin is nonmaleficence: instructors also ensure that students' classroom or field experiences do not cause harm. For example, developmentally appropriate activities and assignments should be used in an effort to promote student growth and protect clients who may be working with students in the field (e.g., practicum, internship).

Instructors also should provide instruction with fidelity. In other words, instructors must be dependable and loyal to their students. It is important that students be able to count on their instructors, relying on their guidance and support during difficult or challenging times. Fidelity supports optimal growth and development, setting the stage for students to maximize their potential in the helping professions.

Finally, instructors must remain conscious that all students are not created equally. Students possess and bring to the learning environment an abundance of knowledge, attitudes, and skills, as well as a variety of experiences. Instructors should access these attributes and empower students in the online learning environment. By emphasizing strengths and differentiating support based on need, a just classroom will be established where all students will thrive.

The guiding principles of ethical behavior, as just outlined, are embedded in a brief Statement of Professional Ethics approved in 2009 by the American Association of University Professors (AAUP, 2009). In addition, an article published by the American Association of Higher Education and Accreditation (Murray, Gillese, Lennon, Mercer, & Robinson, 1996) outlined a series of specific and practical principles for ethical instructors. The article, titled "Ethical Principles for College and University Teaching," emphasized:

- Maintaining a high degree of proficiency in knowledge of subjects taught.
- Upholding and demonstrating competence in pedagogy and instructional practices.
- Handling sensitive issues and subjects in a professional, respectful manner.
- Fostering student development through intentional course design.
- Building solid instructor–student relationships that are driven by academic curriculum.

- Maintaining confidentiality and respecting each student's right to privacy.
- Interacting with colleagues in a professional, respectful manner.
- Ensuring that instructors measure student performance through the use of appropriate assessments.
- Ensuring that instructors adhere to the mission, policies, and goals of the university.

These principles are specific, yet generally comprise ethical behaviors of faculty from all academic units at a university. Instructors in preparation programs that train students to become helping professionals are encouraged to adhere to these ethical standards. Additionally, these instructors also are charged with maintaining behaviors that align with their professional code of ethics.

◼ Ethical Standards Across the Helping Professions

Essentially, all helping professions maintain a set of ethical standards that all members of the respective profession subscribe to. The various codes of ethics across the helping professions are similar, yet also quite different. These codes are typically updated every 5 to 7 years in order to stay relevant and applicable to the ever-changing society and ways in which helping professionals practice. In many cases, codes of ethics are responsive in nature, responding to emerging problems and technological advances. Because of this process, it is likely that you will encounter a dilemma that may be only vaguely referenced in the code of ethics. Such situations lead the professional to use the code's "broad strokes" to infer what is implied in them.

Professional codes of ethics can and should be applied to teaching and the delivery of online instruction. There are a number of ethical standards which align with or speak to the ways in which educators and students should behave in preparation programs. In 2014, the American Counseling Association (ACA) outlined a number of standards in its *Code of Ethics* that translate to or have implications for online instruction.

THE ACA ETHICAL STANDARDS INCLUDE:

- B.1.b. Respect for Privacy
- B.1.c. Respect for Confidentiality
- B.3.c. Confidential Settings
- B.3.e. Transmitting Confidential Information
- B.6.c. Permission to Record
- B.6.d. Permission to Observe
- F.5.b. Impairment

Similarly, in social work, the National Association of Social Workers (NASW, 2008) includes in its *Code of Ethics* sections that are directly related to online education. The NASW ethical standards include:

1.03 Informed Consent

1.03e Electronic Media

1.03f Audiotaping, Videotaping and Third-Party Observation

1.04 Competence

1.07 & 2.02 Privacy and Confidentiality (of clients and colleagues)

2.07 Education and Teaching (in seated and online courses)

Although this list is not comprehensive and only highlights counselor and social work education, all regulated helping professions have a code of ethics that guides the field. Training programs that prepare psychologists, marriage and family therapists, and gerontological counselors, for example, must consider the application of their respective codes of ethics. Additional professional codes of ethics can be found here:

American Association for Marriage and Family Therapy: www.aamft.org/iMIS15/AAMFT/Content/Legal_Ethics/Code_of_Ethics.aspx

American Psychological Association: www.apa.org/ethics/code/

National Association for Professional Gerontologists: www.napgerontologists.org/code_of_ethics.html

The principles and guidelines in these codes should not be abandoned in the online environment. Because of the experiential and reflective nature of courses offered in counselor training programs, these standards and potentially others must be considered. Instructors are encouraged to place ethical practice at the forefront of coursework. By applying these standards and modeling ethical behavior, the instructor enhances the experiences of the students and supports the induction of students grounded in ethical practice into the profession.

Each of these professional programs has a code of ethics that speaks to, at the very least, the need for privacy, confidentiality, and consent. The helping professions rely on the ability to gain the trust of, and build rapport with, clients. It is essential to the helping process to be able to provide a safe environment in which clients can begin the therapeutic process. The classroom is where these practice behaviors are developed and demonstrated. Therefore, it is imperative that privacy be extended and confidentiality be protected as part of the training process in the online environment.

These tenets are not unique to the online or hybrid experience and extend to course work delivered in all formats, including face-to-face courses; however, instructors must attend to them differently in the online milieu. In seated classes, it is much easier and almost, dare we say, natural to guide students through ethical dilemmas and address ethical issues as they arise. In an online class, it is not so natural and often the redirection does not occur as close to the infraction as would be desirable. For instance, most online instructors do not sign onto their class daily but have a set schedule for checking in on the class and discussion boards. So, if a student admits to (or if the instructor *finds out about it* later) an unethical behavior on a Friday and the instructor signs in on Monday to see it, addressing a "cold" issue may be a problem, as many of the students have already seen it and moved on. In a seated class, in contrast, such an unethical behavior could be dealt with quickly, with everyone present. In the online environment, the instructor has to make a blanket statement to make sure that all students are aware of and understand the infraction and the correct way to address the issue.

An example comes from a student in my online class a few semesters ago, who mentioned "When I was talking to my roommate about what [another classmate] said happened at [named local nonprofit] and how three executive directors have left due to the board chair's micromanaging and lack of fiscal knowledge, [the roomate] said that the funder should be called and looked up the contact information." The rest of the post went on to discuss the need for board members to be knowledgeable about nonprofit finances. Although the student was absolutely right that board members have a fiduciary responsibility and should be knowledgeable in this area, the roommate's having enough information to find a phone number and the idea that an intern should call the funder had to be addressed. Because the post was entered over the weekend, the instructor had to send an email addressing the issue in the forum post.

■ Ethical Considerations for Instructors

Somewhat related to the situation just described, there are issues related to the permanence of content developed on the Internet (Bossewitch & Sinnreich, 2013). When content is placed on the Internet, it lives in the ether long after it is deleted or "taken down." I once had a student write a snarky discussion board post about his inability to use one of the course management system features and how I was so unfair for suggesting that he contact the help desk for assistance instead of allowing him to turn it in using a different format outside the learning management system (LMS). He deleted the comment but did not realize that I could still see it even though it was marked as deleted. Because the comment was quite frankly disrespectful, I asked for a meeting. When I asked him if this is what he meant to say and in that way, it was clear that he had no idea I could still see the comment even though he had deleted it.

That example is a relatively low-stakes experience. However, students in the helping professions have to realize that this idea of virtual article permanence is especially relevant. Appropriate self-disclosure and engaging in measures to keep information confidential is particularly important. Understanding how much to share, when to use pseudonyms, and when to change other identifying information when sharing should be addressed early in the term. In helping profession courses, students are faced with responding to discussion threads that may require the sharing of sensitive information. This is much different and far more permanent than discussions held in face-to-face classes. Things like screenshots, snips, and grabs make it possible for information to leave the LMS. Therefore, the expectations regarding class confidentiality have to be stressed.

■ Accountability to Learning

Due to the nature of helping professions, interpersonal skills are essential. Practitioners must have excellent communication and interpersonal skills. The ability to engage in active listening and demonstrate appropriate body language and other nonverbal communication is essential to effective practice. However, these are the most difficult aspects of the online environment to master and assess.

In the face-to-face classroom environment, the ability to demonstrate and assess these behaviors is not difficult. Instructors are literally able to see if students are demonstrating specific competencies. However, in the online environment, the ability to hear voice inflections, see facial expressions, and give and receive nonverbal feedback is limited. For instance, in the classroom, didactic exercises that require students to pair with a classmate and role-play the professional and client interaction require nothing more than moveable chairs. In online classes, the ability for role play and demonstrations is hindered by the online medium and by time. One of the most valuable features of an online asynchronous environment is that students do not have to coordinate schedules to meet at a specific time. The ability to have students participate in activities online may require a certain degree of synchronous activity or creativity on the part of the instructor.

Academic Dishonesty

The topics discussed so far are some of the more nuanced ethical issues related to teaching online. However, a reasonable and often cited concern for instructors considering online education is academic integrity—cheating. In this section, we will discuss academic integrity in a very frank manner. We recommend that instructors do the same when teaching online.

Several research teams (Bedford, Gregg, & Clinton, 2011; Chiesl, 2007) have described concerns related to cheating, testing integrity (Meine, Dunn, & Abbey, 2012), and dishonesty of students in online learning environments. This is concerning, as graduates of programs go on to provide specialized mental health services that they may not be adequately trained to provide if they cheated in their courses.

While instructors would like to believe that students enrolled in helping professions would take integrity seriously and subscribe to ethical behavior, unfortunately that is not always the case. To our chagrin, students cheat. Students cheat in creative and not so creative ways and the online instructor must be proactive in helping students understand what constitutes cheating so that students can avoid it.

To help avoid cheating, in a synchronous class, instructors may have all students open an online exam at once as a timed assessment. Another option for a synchronous or hybrid course would be to have all students come to campus or a testing location on a specific time and date to take a proctored exam. However, in asynchronous online classes, the issue of testing integrity is particularly complex. If the class is fully asynchronous, having scheduled testing times diminishes the flexibility of the class format. Thus, decisions about the format and methods to discourage academic dishonesty must be made after careful consideration.

In the online environment, *unauthorized aid* must be clearly defined by the instructor. By default, the entire Internet is available to students engaged in online education. As a result, instructors must make their expectations for use of the Internet clear and transparent. Are students allowed to look up definitions? Examples? Online tools? Is it acceptable for students to collaborate in person if they take an online class? Can they compare information and notes? Can they provide templates to one another offline?

As the instructor, you have to determine the boundaries for when student collaboration becomes an integrity violation. Then you must communicate those boundaries and expectations to students.

Plagiarism and Student Rights

There are nuances related to the submission of assignments to programs or software that detect plagiarism (Brinkman, 2013). It may potentially violate students' rights when instructors, rather than students, use this type of software. It is important to consult with university offices such as Student Affairs and Academic Affairs prior to using this type of software, especially if it has not been sanctioned by the university. If approval for use is granted, it is still important to understand the policies and processes around its use. While instructors should strive to ensure academic integrity, they must aim to protect students' rights too.

■ Academic Integrity, Ethical Dilemmas, and Students

Essentially all universities have policies in place that address academic integrity. In most instances, instructors are required to include these policies or codes or reference of such in all syllabi. Academic honesty codes vary in depth and breadth across institutes of higher education. An excellent example of a well-designed, comprehensive academic integrity/honor code is that of American University (www.american.edu/academics/integrity/code.cfm). Regardless of the length of the document, several key aspects remain constant: a list of potential violations, due process, and consequences that range from a warning to dismissal from the university.

To diminish the likelihood of academic dishonesty, instructors may engage in discussions about professional ethics statements as well as the university's honor code. (For more information about honor codes and student honor pledges, see Chapter 9.)

The North Carolina State University (NCSU) honor code reads as follows:

Academic Integrity Pledge

Plagiarism is defined as copying the language, phrasing, structure, or specific ideas of others and presenting any of these as one's own, original work; it includes buying papers, having someone else write your papers, and improper citation and use of sources. When you present the words or ideas of another (either published or unpublished) in your writing, you must fully acknowledge your sources. Plagiarism is considered a violation of academic integrity whenever it occurs in written work, including drafts and homework, as well as for formal and final papers.

The North Carolina State University Policies, Regulations, and Rules on Student Discipline (https://studentconduct.dasa.ncsu.edu/code) ultimately set the standards for academic integrity at this university and in this course. Students are expected to adhere to these standards. Plagiarism and other forms of academic dishonesty will be handled through the university's Office of Student Conduct and may result in failure for the project or for the course.

Pledge:

I have read and understood the above statement and agree to abide by the standards of academic integrity in the NC State Policies, Regulations, and Code of Student Conduct.

Students are asked to sign and date a copy of the pledge. Not only does this remind students of the need for ethical behavior, it defines plagiarism, which is a common integrity violation on college campuses.

NC State also encourages instructors to have students include the following "Pack Pledge" on each assignment: "I have neither given nor received unauthorized aid on this test or assignment."

WORD TO THE WISE: Review your university's academic honor code and include it in your LMS and/or your syllabus for students to read. If you are offering a synchronous session, reiterate the policies and guidelines of the honor code in the first session.

Comparable Coursework

As has been noted in earlier chapters, it is not adequate to simply take the information from a seated class, post it online, and expect the class to run the same. Instead, instructors must ensure that online instruction is as effective as and comparable to face-to-face course content (Meine et al., 2012).

In the seated classroom, there are several exercises that require students to reflect in real time; students are presented with a scenario or new information that they then have to reflect upon and give feedback. For example, an exercise prompts students to consider the etiology of a social problem. In class, the students are asked to develop activities of an intervention and encouraged to call out strategies that address the problem, and the instructor records them on one side of the board. Once the students have identified a plethora of activities, the instructor pulls down the screen to cover up those interventions. The instructor then asks, what are the causes of the problem that the intervention is designed to address? Again, students call out the root causes of the social problem. When class reaches saturation, the instructor reveals the previously identified activities and asks the students to match the activities that are relevant to the identified causes. This is a powerful exercise which demonstrates that, invariably, there are activities that do not have a cause. This demonstration is used to discuss how legislation and policy are often developed without addressing the cause of the problem and are not rooted in research regarding the problem or etiology of the social problem.

To convert this to an online activity, students were asked to do the same thing at the prompting of a video. They were asked to take out a sheet of paper. Fold it in half lengthwise, and write the activities on a piece of paper, then turn it over face down. On the clean side, brainstorm the causes. Students were then instructed to open the paper and draw lines from the causes side to the activities side. Finally, students were asked to post to the discussion board about the experience.

In the video prompt, the instructor prompted students with "No, seriously, get a piece of paper. I will wait . . . [whistling while waiting for about 15 seconds]. Need more time, pause the recording. Seriously, get a piece of paper and fold it in half."

It worked! The responses to the discussion were exactly the same as those in the seated class.

■ Opportunities for Practice

Many of our colleagues in the helping professions have been skeptical of online education's ability to ensure that students receive appropriate opportunities for practice prior to contact with clients. The signature pedagogy of social work is the field internship, where students demonstrate the skills and behaviors they learned in the classroom. It makes social work instructors a little more than squeamish when we think of sending unprepared social workers into the field without adequate opportunities to practice the skills they have read about in their textbooks. More specifically, it violates the ethical principle of beneficence. Instructors teaching online have to create experiences for students to demonstrate mastery of course content. Having students record and submit role-play scenarios is particularly effective for assessing student behavior and mastery in an environment that is similar to the seated class. (For tips on how to do role-play exercises in an online environment, see Chapters 8 and 9.)

■ Ethical Decision-Making Models

Ethical dilemmas can lead to stress, create "knots in your stomach," and keep you up at night. These factors can easily blur your perceptions of the situation and can cloud your ability to make sound, rational judgments. Fortunately, a number of decision-making models exist that can aid you in taking appropriate courses of action when dilemmas arise. A quick query of Google will yield thousands of results on the topic. Most members of the helping professions rely on the ethical decision-making model endorsed and promoted by their profession's flagship association. As such, counselor educators often rely on the work of Holly Forester-Miller and Thomas E. Davis (1996). Social workers often refer to the "Essential Steps for Ethical Problem Solving" based on the work of Joseph and Conrad (n.d.). Regardless of your professional affiliation, ethical decision-making models are designed to assist in responding to dilemmas in thoughtful, intentional ways. Most decision-making models are grounded in five key principles (e.g., autonomy, justice, beneficence, nonmaleficence, and fidelity) and espouse comparable processes for problem-solving choice selection.

A general decision-making model is outlined as follows:

1. Determine the perceived problem or ethical dilemma.
2. Refer to your profession's code of ethics.
3. Explore plans or options for addressing the dilemma.
4. Weigh consequences and outcomes of each plan.
5. Identify the best option for addressing the dilemma.
6. Consult with a trusted colleague or peer about the issue and your process for arriving at the selected plan.
7. Adjust/tweak the plan as needed based on the consultation.
8. Implement the plan.
9. Reflect on the process and outcome.

It is important to document the decision-making process, the plan that was carried out, and the outcomes of the plan. In some instances, unintended consequences may occur or the expected outcomes may not come to fruition. However, adhering to a decision-making model that incorporates your profession's code of ethics offers solid footing for the decision that you made and the actions you took.

Consultation from colleagues and peers is often a critical step in the decision-making process. Colleagues can offer a different perspective on the problem and suggest alternative or modified actions for approaching the dilemma. Reflection should not be overlooked, and will always serve to inform decision-making efforts during future ethical dilemmas.

Scenarios for Consideration

Read each scenario. Using an ethical decision-making model, determine if there are ethical or academic integrity concerns. Are there questions for which you would like answers? Finally, explain how you might handle the situation.

1. A student submitted a paper to meet a requirement for a research course you are teaching. You learn that sections of the same paper were submitted by the student the previous semester.

    _____

    _____

    _____

2. As an instructor of the helping skills course, you decide this semester to share with your class a skills demonstration video assignment that a student submitted last semester.

    _____

    _____

    _____

3. You have concerns about the professional disposition of a student enrolled in her last semester of the clinical mental health counseling program. When you address the concern with the student, she begins to cry and promises to address the issue if you just pass her so she can graduate. You agree.

    _____

    _____

    _____

4. You learn from a credible source that a student enrolled in one of your courses is paying someone else to complete the assignments. You are unable to substantiate the claim.

    _____

    _____

    _____

5. You are inundated with papers to grade at the end of the semester. As a result, you elect to give every student full credit for a major course assignment rather than reading, providing feedback, and grading each one.

    _____

    _____

    _____

TAKEAWAYS

1. Make expectations for academic behavior explicit. Review them with students at the beginning of the course and consider reiterating them in advance of assignments and assessments.

2. If there is an issue with ethical behavior, address it immediately and follow through. Instructors should not expect students to engage in questionable behaviors. However, when we see it, we cannot ignore it. Although it is sometimes easier to let it slide, it is not in the best

interests of the student, your own integrity, or the integrity of the profession to allow unethical behaviors in the next generation of helping professionals.

3. Acknowledge that there will be gray areas and that not all academic dishonesty is easy to spot. Be sure to consult with your colleagues, department rules, and university regulations to find out when lines have been crossed and the best way to handle a violation. Use the resources of the Office of Student Conduct (or its equivalent on your campus) and legal services to guide the responses to any violations of policy or ethics.

HELPFUL TIP: Make yourself aware of the process for addressing academic integrity issues before you have to engage in the process. You will feel more secure in addressing these issues if you know how.

"The first step in the evolution of ethics is a sense of solidarity with other human beings."—Albert Schweitzer

Resources

American Counseling Association. Code of ethics. (2014). Retrieved from https://www.counseling.org/docs/ethics/2014-aca-code-of-ethics .pdf?sfvrsn=4

Ethics and Compliance Initiative: www.ethics.org/home

International Center for Academic Integrity: www.academicintegrity.org

Markkula Center for Applied Ethics: www.scu.edu/ethics

References

American Association of University Professors. (2009). *Statement of professional ethics.* Retrieved from https://www.aaup.org/report/statement-professional-ethics

American University. (n.d.). Academic integrity code. Retrieved from http://www.american.edu/academics/integrity/code.cfm

Bedford, D. W., Gregg, J. R., & Clinton, S. M. (2011). Preventing online cheating with technology: A pilot study of remote proctor and an update of its use. *Journal of Higher Education Theory and Practice, 11*(2), 41–58. Retrieved from http://www.na-businesspress.com/JHETP/BedfordWeb.pdf

Bossewitch, J., & Sinnreich, A. (2013). The end of forgetting: Strategic agency beyond the panopticon. *New Media & Society, 15*(2), 224–242. doi:10.1177/1461444812451565

Brinkman, B. (2013). An analysis of student privacy rights in the use of plagiarism detection systems. *Science and Engineering Ethics, 19*(3), 1255–1266. doi:10.1007/s11948-012-9370-y

Chiesl, N. (2007). Pragmatic methods to reduce dishonesty in web-based courses. *Quarterly Review of Distance Education, 8*(3), 203–211.

Forester-Miller, H., & Davis,T. E. (1996). *A practitioner's guide to ethical decision making.* American Counseling Association. Retrieved from https://www.counseling.org/docs/default-source/ethics/practioner%27s-guide-to-ethical-decision-making.pdf?sfvrsn=0

Joseph, V., & Conrad, A. P. (n.d.). *Essential steps for ethical problem-solving.* National Association of Social Workers. Retrieved from http://www.naswma.org/?100

Meine, M. F., Dunn, T. P., & Abbey, R. (2012). Ethical, academic, and practical considerations for online teaching: Does the search for quality and integrity come at the expense of academic freedom? *Internet Learning, 1*(1), Article 6. Retrieved from http://digitalcommons.apus.edu/internetlearning/vol1/iss1/6

Murray, H., Gillese, E., Lennon, M., Mercer, P., & Robinson, M. (1996). *Ethical principles for college and university teaching.* Retrieved from: https://www.aahea.org/articles/Ethical+Principles.htm

National Association of Social Workers. (2008). *Code of ethics.* Washington, DC: Author

CHAPTER 12

Building Community Through Intentional Design: A Course Model

Bethany Virginia Smith and Jakia Salam

OVERARCHING QUESTIONS

1. How do you bring a real-life group counseling session online?
2. What process can you follow to develop an online group counseling course?
3. How can you bring experiential learning into a fully online course?
4. How do you build an online community of learners?
5. How can you incorporate active learning strategies to engage students?
6. What technologies will help you to achieve these goals?

The Distance Education and Learning Technology Applications (DELTA) staff collaborated with a College of Education faculty member to convert the existing version of ECD 539: group counseling course to a fully online distance education (DE) course. This course is a graduate-level course that prepares students to be professional counselors. "DELTA's role within the Office of the Provost is to foster the integration and support of learning technologies in North Carolina State's academic programs, both on the campus and at a distance" (https://delta.ncsu.edu/about/delta).

The team, composed of the faculty member and several DELTA professionals, worked on an innovative solution to create an online environment that facilitated group counseling sessions securely and confidentially. These two factors were paramount in creating an online environment where students can experience group counseling education as they would in a face-to-face setting. This element was crucial in creating a successful online course that provided the necessary experiential learning to the students comparable to experiences in a traditional face-to-face setting.

Another goal of the project was to build and cultivate online learning community. These communities are defined as communities of practice (CoPs; Wenger, McDermott, & Snyder, 2002, p. 104). They "are groups of people who share a concern or a passion for something they do and learn how to do it better as they interact regularly."

When students are online, they can feel as if they are on their own, without facilitated interaction by the instructor. In an online environment "there is greater possibility for a sense of loss among learners—loss of contact, loss of connection, and a resultant sense of isolation" (Palloff & Pratt, 2007, p. 31). Different strategies were adopted to build a robust online student community.

Due to the nature of this course, it was essential to create a safe and secure learning environment where students could share their life experiences and learn from each other. We looked for ways to make students comfortable with the online environment and to build trust among them.

■ Overcoming Student Fear and Anxiety

Online students may be fearful of sharing personal experiences and revealing their true feelings. To overcome this fear factor, we created opportunities for students to engage in different types of icebreaker activities. The first online synchronous collaborative session was designed to help students understand the course structure, expectations, and general information about the course. There was also an opportunity to provide interactions between the student and the instructor and students with each other.

Facilitating the sharing of these experiences in a confidential and secure environment was paramount. Due to the nature of this course, students needed to share their very personal experiences in life, which sometimes can be quite sensitive. The technology selected for use kept this information both private and confidential.

■ Highlights of Instructional Challenges and Solutions

The group counseling course was designed to instruct students on how to conduct counseling sessions in a group setting. Bringing the students together online was a major component of this course. In this chapter we focus on four major instructional challenges:

- Building of an online community
- Development of a safe environment for students
- Experiential learning
- Active learning strategies

Technology played a vital role in our course design. Different learning technologies were investigated and explored that facilitated experiential learning in an online environment. At North Carolina State University, Moodle is our adopted learning management system (LMS). When selecting the technology, we considered these factors:

- Ease of use
- Comfort level with both faculty and student
- Accessibility
- Ease of maintenance in the future by faculty
- Available university support and training
- Well-documented user guide and instructions

▪ Building of an Online Community

Building an online community can be challenging. It takes a good deal of effort, planning, and effective use of instructional design strategies to create a sound and robust online community. One of the primary challenges of creating an online course is to provide an efficient, enjoyable, and comfortable learning environment for both the students and the instructors. Building an online community also creates a "social presence" without physical proximity among instructor and students. *Social presence* is defined as the "degree of salience of the other person in the interaction and the consequent salience of the interpersonal relationships" (Short, Williams, & Christie, 1976, p. 65). This social presence can be difficult to translate to an online environment without deliberate considerations.

We used asynchronous discussion tools in and outside of Moodle to build an online community of learners and foster social presence within the course. Two different technologies were used for asynchronous discussions: Moodle Forum and VoiceThread. Moodle Forum is an effective way for students to share information across a course, and we used it as a tool for traditional posts; VoiceThread was used for asynchronous audio-based discussions around a question or topic.

Asynchronous discussion forums, such as Moodle Forum, are one of the most popular ways to engage students in the class, especially for online and blended learning environments. Students have the flexibility of time and place to reflect on the previous postings to the thread and this encourages engagement with meaningful, intellectual conversation.

In this course, discussion forums were posted during the first week of class to promote interaction between students, between the students and instructor, and between the course content and the students. These forums were critical to establishing a community of practice in the course.

We used VoiceThread for weekly discussions. It is an interactive multimedia, cloud-based tool that enables users to upload images, videos, and documents. The platform allows recorded conversations, both audio and video, to simulate a face-to-face conversation while having the advantages of asynchronous communication.

Researchers conducted a study on self, peer, and instructor critique using VoiceThread as a tool. Their findings demonstrate that high levels of usefulness, usability, motivation, interest, engagement, social presence, and a certain level of reflection are produced when VoiceThread is used as a teaching tool (Gao, Li, Luo, & Smith, 2012). The students appreciate being able to express their own communication style; we found that those who are more extroverted used videos more and those who are more introverted used text comments more.

In this course, VoiceThread was used by the faculty to mimic an in-person discussion. The instructor created a VoiceThread forum around the weekly topic or question and invited students to make audio comments expressing their thoughts on the topic. This provided a more natural discussion platform, and the students responded positively.

VoiceThread can pose some problem if the discussion group is too big. The comments can stack on top of each other and at some point it can be difficult to track postings and responses. In those cases, we recommend either creating smaller VoiceThread groups for discussion around the same topic or using the Moodle Forum. The Moodle threaded discussion forum can be more easily organized and simpler to read. We recommend that you consider the purpose of your discussion forum and use the right tool for the task.

■ Develop a Safe Environment for Students

Building trust and relationship is a challenge in an online environment when there is little or no in-person contact. The unfamiliar territory, new practices, new people, and new skills of online education make it hard for students to know how to engage because of the lack of shared references and general body language communication (Wenger et al., 2002, p. 153). One of the major challenges for a group counseling course is to ensure that students can start interacting and trusting each other from day one. How do we build trust in an online course? We designed some icebreaker activities that facilitate students getting to know each other.

- **One word:** Students think of a word that best describes them. They post their word as the subject of the discussion board posting and then explain why they chose that word in the body of the posting. After all have posted, students review and find someone whose word resonates with them. They reply and try to find at least two additional nouns that the two of them have in common (Conrad & Donaldson, 2010).

- **Introduce yourself:** Students were asked to post one paragraph about themselves and read the other students' posts. This can be translated into a quiz that students earn bonus points for completing in a certain time. For example, you can ask them "Who has a minor in psychology?" or "Who has a white cat?" We adopted this strategy in our project and it was very well received by students. Students also had an option to create a short video to introduce themselves and upload it in the discussion forum.

- **Personality test:** Students take the Myers–Briggs test (www.onlineper-sonalitytests.org/mbti) and share their results with their classmates. They created groups based on their personality types and shared ideas as to what they needed to work on to communicate effectively. A Moodle discussion forum was used to facilitate this conversation.

In the first week of class, a synchronous Blackboard Collaborate session was held with the faculty to facilitate course orientation and discuss the expectations of and guidelines for the class. This "real-time" event allowed students to meet the instructor and their peers.

In this synchronous session, it was made clear that all of their sensitive information would be secure and confidential. All group counseling sessions were password-protected, and required a unique authentication for each student in the class to attend. The students also signed a form of agreement to keep the information discussed in these sessions confidential. This helped to create a "trusted environment" where students were more comfortable in sharing their information.

Experiential Learning

In an experiential learning environment, students learn from doing and sharing their experiences with each other. For students to learn from their experience there should be a conversational space, where students can reflect and talk about their experience together (Kolb, 1984, p. 41). According to Burnard (2013), there are three aspects of experiential learning:

1. Personal experience
2. Reflection on that experience
3. The transformation of knowledge and meaning as a result of that reflection

In the group counseling course, we used various technologies to adapt and support this experiential learning model. Students were encouraged to share their personal experiences, reflections, and ideas.

Blackboard Collaborate: Group Counseling Sessions Online

Group counseling sessions help students get real-world counseling experience and practice conflict resolution, so they are an indispensable part of career education. Our greatest instructional challenges for this course were facilitating experiential learning of group counseling techniques while ensuring confidentiality of content and shared information.

Technology was selected based on faculty and student comfort level, available technical support, and training from the institution. Due to the nature of counseling, the level of security and confidentiality was also a large contributing factor. We compared three technologies: Blackboard Collaborate, Google Hangout, and Adobe Connect. In the end, Blackboard Collaborate, the primary synchronous learning management system (SLMS) at the university, was selected.

During the group counseling synchronous sessions, students were assigned into small online groups. By the end of the semester, every student would have acted as moderator as well as a participant in a mock counseling session. The faculty observed and monitored these sessions and provided guidance when needed.

HELPFUL TIP: When planning synchronous sessions in an online class, we recommend that days and times be explicitly stated in the course catalog or syllabus. Despite being an online class, if synchronous is an integral part of your online teaching, students need to be available at specific dates and times.

After each group counseling session, the students wrote a reflective journal based on the experience they had in the session. Based on their reflective journal, students were asked to conduct an in-depth analysis of their experience and share through the Moodle Forum.

Active Learning Strategies and TPACK

Active learning strategies are an essential pedagogical practice in the counseling education profession. These strategies include active discussions, small group work, Q&A sessions, and the like. Our challenge was to bring some of these strategies to the online environment.

We wanted the online class participants to be actively engaged with the content, rather than be passive receivers of knowledge. It is easy for the instructor to post instructional materials online, test students on their knowledge of the materials, and be done with the course—but do the students actually learn anything this way? How do we encourage the higher order thinking skills (HOTS) that are necessary for students to retain the information that is vital to the program and apply them in their future careers? It was important that we balance the dissemination of knowledge about the content with engaging strategies that build students' understanding.

As instructional designers, we needed to start with our course objectives and content acquisition goals, then we could move to the pedagogical practices that best supported those goals and objectives, as well as the technology that supported both the content knowledge acquisition and the pedagogical strategies (see Figure 12.1). This Technological Pedagogical Content Knowledge Model (TPACK) allowed us to think about choosing the appropriate tools to support student learning (Koehler & Mishra, 2009, pp. 60–70). If discussion was a necessary pedagogical strategy, what tools would help facilitate the discussion we would like to have online? One important feature of the course is that not all discussions have to be treated in the same way, and not all discussions have to be had on a weekly basis strictly in a written forum.

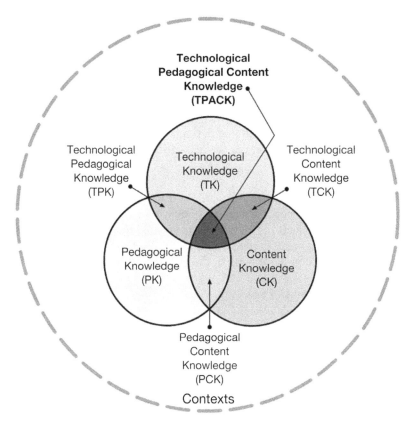

Figure 12.1 Technological Pedagogical Content Knowledge Model (TPACK).
Source: Reproduced by permission of the publisher, © 2012 by tpack.org

■ Tools and Resources to Promote Intentional Design

Moodle

Moodle is an open-source LMS. It provides an online web presence and re-pository that facilitates the delivery of effective online courses.

At North Carolina State University, Moodle is the primary LMS and is self-hosted by the institution. Moodle enables instructors to create, design, and organize a course; add content and media elements; create assessments; build activities; and track grades in a gradebook. It also provides tools for effective communication and played an important role in building an online learning community through the discussion forum.

We created an "orientation" or "Getting Started" module to acclimate students to the LMS and give them information that would help them feel comfortable in the course. Many elements included in those modules are based on the standards identified in the Quality Matters rubric, including a welcome message from the instructor, a "Moodle book" listing all the guidelines and expectations, and the details of the technology used in this course. Some activities, such as the syllabus quiz and icebreakers, were added to establish boundaries that created a safe and trusted online environment.

We created a clean and easy-to-navigate structure with a consistent look and feel. We used color and iconography to brand and create a welcoming environment. Our goal was for students to find the things they needed, when they needed them, and we found that designing an easy-to-use interface allows students to relax and focus on the content of the course.

Video Engagement

Instructional videos are popular methods of delivering content online. Instructors use videos to deliver lectures, demonstrate specific techniques, and illustrate interesting course content to their students. In our design project, one of our goals was to determine if students in the course had watched the videos and retained knowledge of the content. We researched and adopted a few tools that let students pause and reflect on videos as they watch.

The tools we selected have embedded mechanisms to continuously assess and provide feedback on student learning and active engagement to the instructors. Thus, they help instructors continually assess how well students are engaging with the videos.

PlayPosit

PlayPosit is an easy-to-use tool where interactive questions, video branching, and rich media can be inserted into the video's timeline to actively engage students. Students can answer questions as they watch the video. Quiz questions can be from multiple choice or free responses.

Figure 12.2 Getting Started screen shot.

WEEK 1: Introduction to Group Work and the Group Counselor

Introduction to Group Work & the Group Counselor

In week 1, we will explore the definitions and process of the group counseling experience. As we consider the group counseling process, you will begin to examine and reflect on your strengths, areas for growth, and experiences you bring into the group counseling session as a facilitator or co-facilitator in the group counseling setting.

Learning Objectives

- Describe and answer the question, "what is group counseling?"
- Evaluate and answer a self-assessment instrument to reflect on their feelings about being a counselor and group leader.
- Exercise group leadership or facilitation styles in a group setting and approaches, including characteristics of various types of group leaders and leadership styles. (course objective)
- Describe and consider the specific group experiences that will impact the way they facilitate a group (i.e. What specific group experiences will impact the way you facilitate a group?).
- Review and be familiar with the standards established by CACREP related to group counseling.

Folder: 1 URLs: 6 Forums: 2 Choice: 1 Files: 4 External tools: 2 Pages: 2 Assignment: 1

Progress: 1 / 17

WEEK 2: Ethical and Legal Issues in Group Counseling and Theories and Techniques of Group Counseling

Ethical & Legal Issues in Group Counseling

In week two, we will explore the ethical and legal issues of group counseling. The American Counseling Association Code of Ethics will be reviewed and discussed related to group work. Additionally, coverage of theories and techniques used in group sessions will be explored.

Figure 12.3 Weeks 1 and 2 screen shots.

MindTap

MindTap from Cengage is used to present students with specific counseling scenarios. Students are required to reflect and discuss questions related to the scenario while watching the video. The students purchase MindTap as part of a textbook. It is a great resource and offers up-to-date coverage of both the "what is" and the "how to" of group counseling. We used real-life group counseling video-based scenarios, and the students interacted through its built-in video quizzing option. The students also used MindTap's discussion forum to reflect and share their points of view about the scenarios.

Vialogues and Watch2Gether

Vialogues lets students have asynchronous discussions around course video content and point to specific times during the video to give their conversation more context. Watch2Gether, in contrast, is a synchronous tool that allows students to remotely watch a video and chat in real time.

Flipgrid

Flipgrid is a website that allows instructors to create "grids" of short discussion-style questions that students respond to through recorded videos. Student can share their thoughts and ideas in 1 minute and less.

Here are some of the best practices for Flipgrid:

- Questions should be short, open-ended, and more qualitative in style.
- Questions should be low stakes to encourage freedom of expression and creativity.
- Use a video response of yourself to model a response for students.
- Make the first question all about your students.

Quizlet

We wanted students to review terms and definitions that are covered in each module to reinforce group counseling concepts. We used a very user-friendly, free online tool called Quizlet. This tool allows users to create flashcard sets and self-check quizzes to reinforce their learning of concepts.

■ Web Conferencing Tools

We used Blackboard Collaborate as our synchronous LMS and primary web conferencing tool. However, there are many tools out there that are easy to use for students to get together and collaborate.

Zoom

Zoom is a cloud-based video conferencing tool that can create online meetings, group collaboration, and group chat. This tool can be an effective medium of communication, especially for online courses that require group meetings and chat often. The basic version is free to use and cross-platform compatible.

Google Hangouts

Google Hangouts is a browser-based video chat tool. For our students, it is available via North Carolina State University, although participants are required to have a Google account. We considered Google Hangouts as another viable option for online group counseling sessions. This very user friendly and popular tool supports up to 15 users. It is great for informal meetings, sessions, or small-group video chats. We preferred Blackboard Collaborate because it is great for formal structured teaching and can support large cohorts.

Conclusion

It can be a daunting process to develop a course online, and particularly diffi-cult to do so with a course that has community engagement and experiential learning at its core. We focused on the learner's needs first, and this primary consideration drove the majority of our decisions. We recommend using the TPACK framework to help plan what technology can support your pedagog-ical and content knowledge. Once you focus on the learning outcomes and experiences of your course, you can start to map the technology that supports those goals.

We are fortunate to have a university that provided core platforms that allowed for flexibility of interaction, and also the ability to experiment with non-enterprise–level tools that met our pedagogical needs.

REFLECTIVE QUESTIONS

How might you infuse engagement and interactivity into your online course? What might this look like for your course?

What technology is available at your school that could help to build community within the online environment?

"Knowledge is power, community is strength and positive attitude is everything."—Lance Armstrong

Resources

Anderson, T. (2004). Towards a theory of online learning. *Theory and Practice of Online Learning, 2,* 109–119. Retrieved from http://citeseerx.ist.psu.edu/viewdoc/download?doi=10.1.1.131.9849&rep=rep1&type=pdf

Anderson, T., & Kanuka, H. (1997). On-line forums: New platforms for professional development and group collaboration. *Journal of Computer-Mediated Communication, 3*(3). doi:10.1111/j.1083-6101.1997.tb00078.x

Brunvand, S., & Byrd, S. (2011). Using VoiceThread to promote learning engagement and success for all students. *Teaching Exceptional Children, 43*(4), 28–37. doi:10.1177/004005991104300403

Godzicki, L., Godzicki, N., Krofel, M., & Michaels, R. (2013). Increasing motivation and engagement in elementary and middle school students through technology-supported learning environments. *Online Submission*. Retrieved from https://pdfs.semanticscholar.org/7f1e/ 1291ed6dd14e693d1de0e89becace6ec76b8.pdf

Hackman, M. Z., & Walker, K. B. (1990). Instructional communication in the televised classroom: The effects of system design and teacher immediacy on student learning and satisfaction. *Communication Education, 39*(3), 196–206. doi:10.1080/03634529009378802

Hung, D., & Nichani, M. (2002). Differentiating between communities of practices (CoPs) and quasi-communities: Can CoPs exist online? *International Journal on E-Learning, 1*(3), 23–29. Retrieved from https://www .learntechlib.org/p/15114

Johnson, D. W., Johnson, R. T., & Smith, K. A. (2006). *Active learning: Cooperation in the college classroom*. Edina, MN: Interaction Book Company.

Johnson, S. D., Aragon, S. R., Shaik, N., & Palma-Rivas, N. (2000). Comparative analysis of learner satisfaction and learning outcomes in online and face-to-face learning environments. *Journal of Interactive Learning Research, 11*(1), 29. Retrieved from https://www.learntechlib.org/d/8371

McCarthy, M. (2010). Experiential learning theory: From theory to practice. *Journal of Business & Economics Research, 8*(5), 131. doi:10.19030/jber .v14i3.9749

McInnerney, J. M., & Roberts, T. S. (2004). Online learning: Social interaction and the creation of a sense of community. *Educational Technology & Society, 7*(3), 73–81. Retrieved from http://www.ifets.info/ journals/7_3/8.pdf

Meyers, C., & Jones, T. B. (1993). *Promoting active learning: Strategies for the college classroom*. San Francisco, CA: Jossey-Bass.

Nichani, M. R., & Hung, D. W. L. (2002). Can a community of practice exist online? *Educational Technology, 42*(4), 49–54. Retrieved from https:// repository.nie.edu.sg/bitstream/10497/13859/3/ET-42-4-49.pdf

Oviatt, S. (2006, October 23–27). Human-centered design meets cognitive load theory: Designing interfaces that help people think. In *Proceedings of the 14th ACM International Conference on Multimedia* (pp. 871–880). Santa Barbara, CA: ACM. doi:10.1145/1180639.1180831

Palloff, M. R., & Pratt, K. (2004). Learning together in community: Collaboration online. In *20th Annual Conference on Distance Teaching and Learning* (pp. 4–6). Retrieved from http://www.uwex.edu/disted/conference

References

Burnard, P. (2013). *Teaching interpersonal skills: A handbook of experiential learning for health professionals.* New York, NY: Springer Science+Business Media. doi:10.1007/978-1-4899-7104-3

Conrad, R. M., & Donaldson, J. A. (2010). *Engaging the online learner: Activities and resources for creative instruction* (Vol. 31). San Francisco, CA: Josey-Bass.

Gao, F., Li, K., Luo, T., & Smith, J. (2012). *Reconsidering instructional design with Web 2.0 technologies.* ODU Digital Commons. Retrieved from http://digitalcommons.odu.edu/stemps_fac_pubs/4

Koehler, M. J., & Mishra, P. (2009). What is technological pedagogical content knowledge? *Contemporary Issues in Technology and Teacher Education, 9*(1), 60–70. Retrieved from http://www.citejournal.org/volume-9/issue-1-09/general/what-is-technological-pedagogicalcontent-knowledge

Kolb, D. A. (1984). *Experiential learning. Experience as the source of learning and development.* New York, NY: Prentice Hall.

Palloff, R. M., & Pratt, K. (2007). *Building online learning communities: Effective strategies for the virtual classroom*(2nd ed., retitled) San Francisco, CA: Josey-Bass.

Short, J., Williams, E., & Christie, B. (1976). *The social psychology of telecommunications.* London, UK: John Wiley & Sons.

Wenger, E., McDermott, R. A., & Snyder, W. (2002). *Cultivating communities of practice: A guide to managing knowledge.* Brighton, MA: Harvard Business Press. Retrieved from http://cpcoaching.it/wp-content/uploads/2012/05/WengerCPC.pdf

CHAPTER 13

Pedagogy and Technology in the Helping Professions: Now and in the Future

VIGNETTE

Imagine 20 years from now: What will online classes, course development, and the instructional process look like? What considerations do you need to think about now while you are designing and teaching your courses that will help your course and programs be sustainable for the future? Also, how will you prepare yourself to remain relevant and current about where the helping professions (such as online counseling, therapy, and instruction) are headed in the future?

OVERARCHING QUESTIONS

1. If there were no limitations to technology and online delivery methods, what would you envision your online course to look like in the future (e.g., virtual reality, connecting anywhere, anytime, role plays in "live" format, supervision in the moment)?

2. How comfortable are you with change and changes in technology, on a scale from 1 to 5 (i.e., 1: I wholeheartedly resist change through 5: I enthusiastically embrace change)?

3. What personal limitations and/or barriers may prevent you from staying current and thinking about the way you will deliver online content or mental health services in the future?

4. What professional organizations and committees can you draw upon for technical exposure and support?

5. What is your plan for staying current with the upcoming technological advances and updates that occur with the systems used in online learning and teaching?

You may be wondering: How am I supposed to stay current in this fast-paced, ever-changing technological movement, especially as a non-techy person?

I will venture to say that most of us within the helping professions do not have a specialty area within computer science or another technical field. However, more and more, we are called on to delivery pedagogy using a variety of technological tools. How do we stay current and forward-thinking?
Here are a few recommendations:

1. Connect with your university's online learning department or office of information technology (i.e., the department that offers workshops, webinars, trainings, and technical support for your courses). Attend the workshops and trainings to test the technology and experiment in a live space with others who are learning just like you.

2. Identify within your content area opportunities where technology has already been used to deliver courses, webinars, workshops, and so forth. Use your professional organizations and divisions that may offer specific support and content around technology and your discipline. For example, within the counseling profession, the American Counseling Association offers a division that specifically focuses on technology and the use of technology within the profession.

3. Attend instructional design conferences outside of your field. Attending cross-discipline and multidisciplinary conferences can be extremely useful and allow you to learn from other fields that may be more technologically advanced than the helping professions. Identify ways to adapt the content shared to your own courses and content area(s).

4. Reach out to other faculty who teach online at your institution. Create a lunch-and-learn to share ideas, experiences, best practices, and other lessons learned.

5. Subscribe to listservs, social media outlets, and publications that highlight new technology that is being developed. Practice, test, and experiment through piloting technology in a small course or through other ways, such as academic advising, scheduling, committee work, and so forth.

At the administration level, decisions about technology can be made with little notification. For example, instructors may be told that the learning management system (LMS) that has been used for years is going to be dropped and the university will be adopting a new system. The implications of this change can be overwhelming for the instructor and students due to the steep learning curve and the addition of new software, process, logistics, and systems.
Here are some things to consider if and when this type of situation occurs at your university:

1. Will the content seamlessly move from one LMS to the new system? What are the issues regarding timing of the changeover?

2. Will content have to be developed and recreated in the new system?

3. What support is offered to learn, test, and practice the new LMS?

4. What is the plan for sharing and disseminating the "rollout" of the new LMS to faculty, staff, and students?

5. How will faculty access the LMS and engage with tech support, if and when issues arise, before, during, and after the semester?

What other considerations might you add to this list?

Ethical Considerations With Technology

It is important to consider ethics, regardless of the tools you embed and use in your online course. As noted in Chapter 11, instructors must remain vigilant in their efforts to provide instruction that meets and adheres to ethical guidelines. With advances in technology occurring so rapidly, codes of ethics likely will not address or encompass all ethical dilemmas that may arise. Decision-making models are invaluable tools that instructors can use to ensure that ethical dilemmas are managed appropriately. It is also important for instructors to take time to understand the tools they are using in classes and exposing their students to. For example, failure to recognize the privacy limitations some of these technologies offer can involve the instructor in an ethical dilemma that could have been avoided.

Licensure and Certification

It is imperative for instructors and helping professionals to be cognizant of the licensure requirements in the state, nation, and internationally for their discipline. Also, certifications are needed related to the delivery method. For example, within the counseling profession, counselors visit the National Board for Certified Counselors website (www.nbcc.org) to peruse literature to remain up-to-date with ethical standards and counseling practice. The ethical standards and codes for social workers are accessible at www.socialworkers.org/pubs/code/default.asp/.

Current and Developing Technology for the Future Blogs

Incorporating written or video blogs into a course can be a great way to keep students engaged and up-to-date on what is occurring in the moment. Instructors can create a blog highlighting class content, logistics, and anything relevant to the course. Students can be asked to write blog entries throughout the semester: as an assignment to track progress, as a way to create private or public journals, and/or as a way to write about a specific topic related to the coursework.

There are many examples of blogs within the helping professions. Here are a few:

- Bloglovin' is a social work blog.

- Making the world a better place—Social Work Helper: www.social-workhelper.com/2017/01/10/10-apps-can-impact-change-world

■ Google Suite

To organize your life, the Google Suite of apps (gsuite.google.com) can help to create lists, organize schedules, track lists, and so forth.

Google Docs is incredibly useful for online classes because they are designed for online use. Information can be embedded in a Google Doc and that document can be embedded in a LMS. It is an efficient way to work in a group or when multiple people are collaborating on a project, because the document is saved online where it can be accessed and edited by all.

Google Docs can be used for creating presentations and sharing documents with others in the class.

WORD TO THE WISE: Google Docs are intended to be used within the online environment and shared within the online framework. Typically, Google Docs are not intended to be printed, but rather act as a collaborative online space to be shared, embedded, and so forth.

I often embed Google Docs in my LMS and ask students to write on the document their views on a particular subject matter. For example, prior to inviting a guest speaker to our synchronous space, I create a Google Doc and add it to the LMS and request students to add questions for the presenter a week prior to the guest speaker's arrival to our session. After all questions are shared on it, I share this document with the guest speakers in advance to help them to prepare for their session.

An instructor can create a Google Doc for students to share their introductions, including pictures, pets, family members, interests, and any information related to the topic for the course.

Get to know the Google Suite! It also includes Google Slides, Google Calendars, Google Sheets, Google Hangout, Gmail, Drive, and more.

■ YouTube

YouTube is far, far more than just a collection of crazy cat videos!

YouTube is a library of amazing, informative, crazy, and even academic videos that can be used as learning tools. With a few keyword searches, you can find videos of professors, practitioners, and video bloggers sharing their expertise; these can easily be used to highlight a concept or current topic in your online class.

Students can make their own YouTube videos to record an introductory video of themselves at the beginning of the semester or program. Students can set the video as private and post the link into the LMS for all classmates to review and comment on. By viewing these videos, students can put a name to a face and begin building rapport with one another.

In the asynchronous platform, a YouTube link can be shared within the LMS. In the synchronous platform, many systems will provide a space where you can add the URL link and the class can all view the video at the same time.

Student Engagement

Poll Everywhere: www.polleverywhere.com
This polling tool can be used to engage students and take the pulse of the class. The instructor can ask a question and solicit a response via the phone or web browser.

VoiceThread: voicethread.com
I considered several tools to provide discussion forums in which students could engage with and respond to one another. My rationale for choosing voicethread was twofold:

1. It allows students to respond to one another using voice, audio, video, text, and uploaded documents, and the replies are threaded.

2. It can be adapted to fit different teaching styles. Instructors who prefer to share pictures or create visuals can upload images into the space and invite students to engage with the content in multimodal ways (e.g., audio, voice, drawing), rather than simply typing out responses as in a typical discussion forum.

Digital Storytelling

Students can use videos to share their own stories, case studies, and/or role plays in the digital platform. One idea could be to create an assignment whereby students share a case conceptualization or the client background for simulated client/therapist interactions. Students can use digital storytelling to share their story or the client's story. The stories could be shared via the LMS within the class to ensure privacy of the information. If given permission by the student, stories could be repurposed in another semester and may serve as excellent teaching aids and/or resources for future students in the course. Selected student stories could be used as examples of exemplary work to help future students create their own stories.

Video Journaling

Students share reflections about the content or how they are feeling through video journals that are uploaded and viewed by the instructors(s). Instructors can provide video feedback in return as a way to personalize the evaluation and comments. Instructors can use Jing or some LMSs that have recording software built into the system.

WORD TO THE WISE: Keep videos within a specified time frame (e.g., less than 5 minutes).

Additional Resources to Explore

1 Second Everyday: 1se.co

Instructors can use this app to post and share a new picture, quote, idea, or thought to track important information throughout the semester related to the content area of the course. For example, when teaching a career development course, adding a helpful career-related tip to the site each day could be a fun way to create connection with your students (e.g., resume tip, cover letter suggestion, interviewing point to remember, networking opportunity, professional development organization).

Convinceme: www.convinceme.net

The Convinceme site provides opportunities for students to debate a topic. This type of site can be useful forto discussing ethical issues and dilemmas. Students can take a specific stance on a topic and debate one side or the other. Convinceme can be added as an extension through Chrome platforms.

Pear Deck: www.peardeck.com

The Pear Deck application enables instructors to share their presentations with their students in an interactive way. Peers can connect and share information with one another as well.

PowToon: www.powtoon.com

Creative, short animated videos can be created with PowToon to share content withto students. PowToon can be used for student presentations as well. Instructors may design PowToon videos to send students introductions to the course, information about the field, professional information, and information on organizations in psychology, social work, marriage and family therapy, counseling, and other helping professional fields.

◼ Interactive Tools

Mindmeister: www.mindmeister.com

The resource can be used for mind mapping and developing ideas for related content.

Kahoot: getkahoot.com

A fun, free, interactive learning tool that engages students and participants through their web browsers or phones. Instructors can create a short game with five to 10 questions and offer four possible responses for students to choose from in the game. Selecting quickly and correctly raises one's level in the game.

Remind app: www.remind.com

The Remind application gives instructors at all levels the opportunity to set schedule reminders for students, student groups, and so forth. Instructors can connect with students through "remind" to share information, remind students about deadlines, inform of advising hours, and so forth.

Answer Garden: answergarden.ch

The application is a tool that elicits feedback and invitees multiple participants to respond to a question.

Voki: www.voki.com

A fun way to create animated presentations. In Voki, you can select an image or even animal and add content as if the image were sharing the content with students.

Quizlet: www.quizlet.com

Many students within the helping professionals will be required to complete national exams for licensure. A way to assist students in remembering key terms and concepts is to create flashcards with words and definitions on applications like Quizlet.

Additionally, creating a glossary of terms related to your specific field and discipline is useful for students to review and quickly flip through when studying and preparing for exams in your class and national exams in the future.

Piazza: piazza.com

This free platform offers an easy, Wiki-style Q&A format. Students can endorse other people's answers and create folders for easy tracking of content.

Vizia: vizia.co

Vizia allows the instructor to embed polling and quizzes into videos or recordings.

■ Recordings, Videos, and Screencasting

Camtasia: www.techsmith.com/camtasia.html

The Camtasia site aids in creating videos and supplies screencasting information for recording lectures and interactive videos.

Mediasite: www.sonicfoundry.com

The Mediasite technology offers live streaming, recording, and video editing within the platform. Instructors can record lectures and stop at various points to ask students questions. Students can also respond to the questions on the Mediasite platform.

Jing: jing.en.softonic.com

Jing technology can be used for screen capturing and short recording to share information verbally with students. Jing can also be used for grading and providing feedback to students. Additionally, students can create screen captures for assignments that involve sharing and presenting material to peers and instructors.

Light boards with video: vital.oit.duke.edu/documentation/video-examples andwww.youtube.com/watch?v=FYwXOLU4TKk

Lightboards are a creative way to engage students during an online lecture. A lightboard uses a clear sheet of glass or plexiglass, a mirror, and video camera. This setup allows the instructor to write on the board while facing the students/camera. It works well for describing formulas and displaying content in an organized way.

Podcasts

Podcasts are audio recordings on a variety of commentary, interviews, and topics. Students can search for relevant podcasts to learn about the discipline. Some podcasts in the helping professions offer suggestions for self-care, relaxation techniques, documentaries and life stories, tips and strategies for success, and so forth.

WORD TO THE WISE: When posting a recording or video, include the length of time or duration of the recording in the label or title so that students can plan ahead before beginning to use the recording.

Presentation Skills

Like So: sayitlikeso.com

A resource to share with students who are interested in observing their language and frequency with which they use certain words. Students can use the app prior to presenting for in-class projects or within practicum or field experiences to develop a greater awareness of the "filler" words used in everyday conversation. For professional development, students can use the app to conduct and practice mock interviews in preparation for real interviews for practicum, internship, and full-time employment.

Piktochart: piktochart.com

Students can use this technology to create quick flyers, brochures, posters, and templates for presentation, by capturing the key information on one page. Instructors can require the submission of a Piktochart to find out how well students can quickly and concisely present the main points of the assignment. The Piktochart can be either an alternative or a supplement to a PowerPoint presentation. The option also helps to eliminate the abundance of words on each slide and creates easily digestible information.

Virtual Reality

360 video: multimedia.journalism.berkeley.edu/workshops/vr
Virtual reality tools can be very useful in the helping professions. Using the tool during role plays and live sessions can help supervisors view the client and therapist within the session using 360-degree technology. A complete view of the session allows the supervisor to see nonverbal communication of both the client and therapist from all angles.

Course Design and Standards

Faculty Focus: Higher Ed Teaching Strategies from Magna Publications: www.facultyfocus.com
This is a weekly, subscription newsletter that offers helpful teaching strategies and tips. Some examples of topics include rubrics, grading, building community, technology reviews, and so forth.

Quality Matters: www.qualitymatters.org
Quality Matters is a resource for instructors and administrators to measure effectiveness of online courses offered at the institution. Quality Matters seeks to improve constancy and develop standards for meeting course design expectations.

Resource Collection

Pinterest: www.pinterest.com
Instructors and students can create boards on various topics related to the helping professions. For example, instructors who teach multiple courses may decide to create a board for each class, which includes resources, links, activities, and other information to share with their students. The resource serves as a permanent location for students to visit even after the course ends. Instructors can ask students to create Pinterest boards to share with one another or create an assignment using the boards to network, share, and/or display relevant information.

WORD TO THE WISE: If you are an avid Pinterest user and have a personal account, it is suggested that you create a professional account for your students so as to keep the two accounts separate. Helping professions can create specific boards and also follow boards related to social work, psychology, counseling, marriage and family therapy, and other helping professions.

▪ Distance Counseling and Therapy

The initiation of online counseling and clinical mental health services is underway. Licensing and certification boards are currently offering opportunities for helping professionals to obtain online certifications for distance counseling credentials. Online mental health counseling services are becoming more popular. For example, Telehealth Certification Institute offers online and onsite certification for learning distance counseling practices.

A few of the distance education certification organizations include both domestic and international certifications for counselors and other helping professionals. The Center for Credentialing and Education offers a Distance Certified Counselor certification. The International Distance Education Certification Center offers specific training for helping professionals who choose to offer mental health services internationally to their clients.

Conferences Related to Online Learning

Magna Teaching Assistant Professor Conference: www.magnapubs.com/2017-teaching-professor-conference
Online Learning Consortium conference: onlinelearningconsortium.org

The American Counseling Association offers a technology interest network, titled the Counseling and Technology Interest Network, for members who may be interested in joining the listserv.

The National Association of Student Personnel Administrators (NASPA) offers a knowledge community related to technology. One resource is the Technology KC Guide for the 2017 NASPA Annual Conference (www.naspa.org/constituent-groups/posts/technology-kc-guide-for-the-2017-naspa-annual-conference).

■ Stay Organized!

The following applications can be useful to get you organized and keep you that way.

Wunderlist: www.wunderlist.com
This application allows you to create lists for specific tasks. You can add each task independently, then check it off the list when completed. The application provides opportunities for sharing lists with others, too.

Calendly: calendly.com
A system that allows you to schedule meetings effortlessly without having to go back and forth with multiple emails.

Doodle: doodle.com
If you need to schedule a meeting with multiple people, using Doodle can help you to schedule without the fuss.

YouCanBook.me: youcanbook.me
This site allows students and colleagues to schedule a time on your calendar to meet with you based on the parameters you set for your schedule.

12 Good Task Management Apps for Teachers: www.educatorstechnology
.com/2017/06/12-good-task-management-apps-for.html

This resource was shared for teachers through Educational Technology and
Mobile Learning. The apps listed can help instructors organize their work and
home lives in an easy, manageable, and systematic way.

TheSkimm: www.theskimm.com
This site publishes a daily newsfeed that boils down the most recent current
events so that you can "skim" it all quickly in one email. Stay current and on
top of the national and international happenings by "skimming" the latest
news to start your day.

TAKEAWAYS

1. Part of an instructor's responsibility is to remain current with technology.
   One constant in the online environment is change.
2. Software will be updated to new and, hopefully, improved versions over
   time, which will enhance features and increase usability.
3. Reminder: Don't be afraid to ask for help and identify technology experts
   who can support your online instruction when the updates occur for
   a LMS or online platform. For example, a change in the structure of a
   gradebook can create challenges at first, but it actually may increase
   productivity, flexibility, and ease of use in the long run.
4. It may appear on the face of it to be overwhelming; however, staying
   current in both the content and process of the helping professions along
   with the technology is a necessity for instructors.

   *"Technology is nothing. What's important is that you have a faith in
   people, that they're basically good and smart, and if you give them
   tools, they'll do wonderful things with them."—Steve Jobs*

Resources

Telehealth Certification Institute: telementalhealthtraining.com

Center for Credentialing and Education (re the Distance Credentialed
Counselor certification): www.cce-global.org/DCC

International Distance Education Certification Center: www.idecc.org

CHAPTER 14

You Are a Helping Professional! You Can Do This: Conclusion and Encouraging Final Thoughts

As we come to the end, we would like to offer you words of encouragement and support as you take off on your exploration and quest into online teaching. Thank you for taking this journey with us! Also, thank you for making an impact on so many lives through your essential role as a helping professional, administrator, and/or online teaching instructor.

■ Jeffrey M. Warren

Online instruction is like a box of chocolates . . . well, not really, but it "is what you make of it." Making it into what I envision it can be requires time, dedication, and in some instances blood, sweat, and tears. However, the benefits of delivering a well-developed, coordinated online course are great, both for you and, most importantly, for your students. As academics, we are lifelong learners by nature and should embrace technology and all it has to offer. Whether you are a digital native or immigrant, the time is now and the resources are in this book to either develop your online course or retool your existing one.

■ Siu-Man R. Ting

Satya Narayana Nadella, the Microsoft CEO, predicts that in the next decade online education will dominate undergraduate education in our country. Given the trend of online education and the increasing evidence of its effectiveness, we can foresee the increase of online education in helping professions as well. Because we may well witness the emphasis on face-to-face education gradually becoming less important in the future, helping profession educators need to grasp the opportunities to develop new online education programs in counseling, social work, psychology, and related professions. Changing is not an easy process. However, in order to advance our professions, we need to embrace the new world of high technology and find ways to get involved to satisfy the needs of the new generations through online education.

It was a bit scary to me 10 years ago when I started to teach my first online counseling course. I was the only person who taught online in our department then. In the process, I have learned a lot and feel fortunate to have received great support from my colleagues, including Dr. Smith and many others. Now, North Carolina State University offers an online master's degree and an online graduate certificate program, with more than 120 students enrolled—more than that in the on-campus programs. The journey will continue so long as we see the needs of the students as well as in our profession.

Jocelyn D. Taliaferro

Ten years ago, as an untenured assistant professor, I dove headfirst into online teaching. I think that was the best thing I could have done. If I had taken more time to think about it, I probably would not have done it! My youth, enthusiasm, and impulsiveness brought me to the world of online teaching and I LOVE it. It's hard work and it requires all of the social work skills I own. I did not have a resource-like book to help guide me along the way. Do not let our cautions scare you! Take them in the context in which they were given: as a road map to avoid our mistakes. I do not consider myself an expert, but I have learned quite a bit in the process.

Angie C. Smith

Reflection is an integral part of the helping professions. Now that we have reached the end of the book, I cannot help but reflect back on our purpose for writing it. One of the main reasons for walking down this path was the experience of my own struggles and challenges as I fumbled to teach content in an ever-changing medium, especially early on in my career. My hope was to provide a resource to help anyone who may feel the way I did (e.g., nervous, overwhelmed, and unsure of how this would all work) when beginning my career as an online instructor. This book will, I hope, serve as a resource, a companion, or perhaps even a sanity check, for those attempting to learn how to teach online. Much like our profession, identifying a guide, support, and/or a resource can make life a lot easier and more enjoyable. My sincere hope for you is that this will provide you with useful information, ideas, and examples for your own practice. I also hope that reflecting with the guided prompts and questions throughout the book will create an interactive experience, rather than a "one-sided" conversation with each reader.

As I think about the helping professions, a quote from one of my childhood favorites, Fred Rogers, embodies the way I feel about our role and what we are able to provide to our clients in the important work we do every day.

"Anything that's human is mentionable, and anything that is mentionable can be more manageable. When we can talk about our feelings, they become less overwhelming, less upsetting, and less scary. The people we trust with that important talk can help us know that we are not alone."

In essence, we are the reader's listeners, helpers, supporters so that no one has to feel alone on the journey. I am grateful for you, the reader, and all the work you so effortlessly pour into your students and clients. You make the world a better place for us all!

As we conclude the final chapter and book, we would like to offer a concluding activity that can be used in a synchronous environment.

■ Mosaic and Wrap-Up

1. Ask students to summarize and/or synthesize their experience into one picture, word, or image (e.g., browse the website for images, while they are online) as they reflect back upon the semester.

2. Place a word or image in the center of the screen/whiteboard and ask students to respond by listing one learning or takeaway they will use in practice or remember in their personal or professional lives.

3. After students share on the board, invite students to reflect on what they shared in breakout rooms, then in the large, main room; or, if time is limited, ask students to share in the large room with all students present.

4. Place students in their own breakout room and invite them to create a picture/image/illustration of their overall class experience, then bring the students back to the large room and copy their page over to the main room. Then, invite students to share their page with their colleagues, as they feel comfortable. The instructor can bring up the individual page for students as they "raise their hands," and students can then elaborate and reflect on why they selected or created the image and the meaning behind it.

REFLECTIVE QUESTIONS

In the following space, share three specific tasks you can initiate after reading the text to support your online learning and/or student learning outcomes. Some guiding questions may be:

1. After reading the text, what samples can you adapt or use for your own course(s)?

2. What resources are most relevant to your work experience at your university, in your department, within your courses, and so forth?

3. What concrete steps can you take before, during, and after offering a course to ensure a smooth and stress-free semester?

Your tasks and next steps:

1. _____
2. _____
3. _____

■ Getting Started Checklist

1. What are your top five goals and/or objectives for your course and/or program?

2. Draw a matrix or roadmap for a success at least 2 to 4 weeks prior to the beginning of the semester (preferably earlier, if possible).

3. Who can support you in reaching and achieving your goals? Who are your cheerleaders and colleagues you can rely on during your challenging days? Have their names, emails, and numbers handy if and when needed.

4. What learning management system (LMS) does your school use? What technology do you need?

5. What training and/or resources do you need to be successful before, during, and after the course is offered?

6. What colleagues have taught your course before or taught in an online environment? Schedule a meeting with them to share and exchange ideas!

7. How do you plan to deliver your content (e.g., asynchronously, synchronously, hybrid)?

8. What do students who will be taking your course need to know about being successful online learners?

■ Planning Timeline Checklist

Congratulations! You have just discovered that you are going to be teaching an online class within the helping professions. Whether you are an instructor in psychology, social work, counseling, marriage and family therapy, or another helping profession, we sincerely hope this book serves as a supportive reference and companion for you as you begin your online teaching journey.

Ideally, in a perfect world, you would have at least a month or more to prepare for your class. In an imperfect world, you will have less time.

Assuming you have the content and textbook selected for the course, here is a template or "cheat sheet" timeline to use as a step-by-step guide to help you deliver your course on time and effectively.

We have indexed steps in the timeline so you can easily find more detailed information in previous chapters to help you on your way.

◼ One Month (or Less) Before the First Day of Class

Planning Phase

Before you can do anything, you need to know the answers to these questions:

- Is this course offered as a hybrid, asynchronous, or synchronous class?
- Identify technical support on your campus.
- What LMS, synchronous platform, and other technology does the university use?
- How many students will be in the course?
- How many credit hours and weeks is the course offered?
- Is the course a required course? What are the specific accreditations or standards relevant to it? How will you keep standards intact online?

Design

- ☐ Discuss with your department if you will be provided an instructional designer to assist you with the design of your course. If so, make friends with the design team.
- ☐ Identify your support system and university's distance learning department.
- ☐ Contact the distance education office to locate your course shell or identify how to copy a preexisting course within the LMS to the new semester.
- ☐ Find out if there is a preexisting syllabus for the format of the online course you will be teaching or if one must be created.
- ☐ Become familiar with the software you will use to teach the course. Use your friends and resources!
- ☐ Research copyright laws and regulations for teaching online and review the Technology, Education and Copyright Harmonization (TEACH) Act of 2002.

Build

- ☐ Build your module: create an outline for your course.
- ☐ Upload the syllabus.
- ☐ Add your university's student honor code to the student center or LMS.
- ☐ Begin adding content and graphics, and organize the material based on dates specified on the syllabus.
- ☐ Build your rubrics, group work activities, and assignments.

☐ Upload or link videos, blogs, websites, activities, and discussion boards.

☐ Test, revamp, and revise. Be sure to check the "student view" on the LMS.

Ten Days Out

☐ Create the Welcome Letter/video for students to get to know you and see you before the synchronous sessions start.

☐ Organize the student center on your LMS.

☐ Develop introduction and icebreaker activities.

☐ Create a way for students to introduce themselves in the student center.

☐ Test all your links, videos, uploaded content, and links students will need to open in the LMS.

☐ Check the student view of the LMS to ensure that they are viewing the content the way you are viewing the content.

☐ Delete or hide any unnecessary buttons that you don't plan on using.

☐ For your synchronous class, develop a detailed script that highlights the lesson plan and material to be covered in the moment along with the procedures.

One Week Out

☐ Send out the Welcome Letter.

☐ Participate in an introductory activity to get to know your students.

☐ Review your plan for tracking student participation.

☐ Double-check that the bookstore has the correct textbook edition and enough copies.

☐ Check that due dates in the calendar and syllabus are correct.

☐ Finish loading and organizing content and activities.

☐ Check that your gradebook is set up correctly (no extraneous columns, total points are correct, etc.).

☐ Stay alert for student requests for accommodations. Depending on the accommodation, it may be helpful to contact your institution's accessibility services department.

The Day the LMS Opens

☐ Email all students to let them know that week 1 is available, and give instructions/reminders on how to access the system.

▪ The First Day of the Semester

4 to 5 Hours Before Class

☐   Log into the LMS and make sure all content is uploaded and ready to go.

15 to 20 Minutes Before Class

☐   Get a glass of water, set up your desk, go to the bathroom, locate your script, and take a few deep breaths.

Go Live!

☐   Welcome participants into the space and say hello in the chat box.

☐   Consider including a link to music for them to stream while they wait for the class to begin.

☐   Press the talk button and begin the class as you would in an on-campus course, and use your script.

☐   Be sure to take attendance in the class if this is part of the final grade.

▪ One Week Into the Semester

☐   Assess: Are your students tracking? Are you settling in? Is something missing from the class?

☐   Reiterate how discussion boards will be graded and provide specific feedback to students in the rubric.

☐   Ensure that assignments have a rubric (where applicable).

▪ Mid-Semester

☐   Assess: students, yourself, your course

☐   Ask for feedback from your students on technology and tools.

☐   Use feedback to rethink and reorganize content and technology for next semester.

☐   Provide midterm grades if applicable.

☐   Make any tweaks to your online course for later weeks.

■ End of Term

☐   Provide students with information about final exams and end-of-semester projects.

☐   Provide final grades to students.

☐   Submit final grades to your institution.

☐   Remind students to do end-of-course evaluations.

☐   Remind students to capture and save any information they would like to keep from the LMS, course, and fellow students.

After Class Ends

☐   Copy any course design changes that you want to keep from your "live" course back to your "play" space, because the "live" course will be archived.

☐   You did it! (We knew you could!) Celebrate! But don't celebrate too long because the next semester starts soon!

HELPFUL TIP: After teaching an online course, celebrate all that has been accomplished. Reflect upon what went well and any changes you would like to make the next time the course is offered. Journal your responses online or in a notebook to track your progress as an online instructor. As you celebrate, remember how many lives you have touched through the vital work that you do within the helping profession on a daily basis to make this world a better place for all who inhabit it!

You can do it! Take a deep breath . . . baby steps, the first step can often be the hardest, but it's essential to the journey.

The beginning is the end and the end is just the beginning . . .

Index

icebreaker activities, 114–115
in vivo role-play, 119
instant messaging. *See* chat/chatting
instructor anxieties, reduction
    strategies
  ABC model of emotional
    disturbance, 25
  consistency, 23–24
  different types of solution, 24–25
  practical strategies, 23
  preparation, 23
  presence and visibility, 23
  technological knowledge, 24
instructor experience
  asynchronous student center, 90
  cyber café or student lounge, 91
  engagement and interactivity,
    students, 96–97
  grades and grading, 101–104
  group work, 93–94
  innovation, 111
  inviting guest speakers, 91–92
  large assignments, 91
  lectures, 92–93
  piloting, 78–79
  professional identity, 99
  researching new technology, 78
  student accessibility, 105–107
  student initiatives, 98–101
  student presentations, 94–96
  synchronous advising sessions,
    104–105
  template creation, 91
  video production, 94
instructors
  academic dishonesty, 147–148
  academic integrity/honor code,
    148–149
  codes of ethics, 143–144
  decision-making models, 151–153
  ethical considerations, 146–147
  instructional challenges and solutions,
    156–157
  opportunities to practice, 150
  plagiarism, 148
  student rights, 148
interactive theory education, 119
interactive tools, 174–175
Internet service provider (ISP), 15
ISP. *See* Internet service provider

Jones, Shenika, 116
JoomlaLMS, 11

Kahoot, 174–175

laptops, 15–16
learning management systems
  assessment and testing, 90
  asynchronous student center, 90
  building process, 61–65
  class confidentiality, 146–147
  course design, 58–59, 88–96
  dyad-client exercise, 87
  end-of-course student video, 118
  grades and grading, 101–102
  group counseling course, 156
  group work, 93
  guest speakers, 92
  online tools, 77–79
  options, 8–14
  quality of feedback, 117
  recorded syllabus, 106
  rules of etiquette, 74
  site access, 83–84
  student presentations, 94–96
  syllabus quiz, 89
  time management, 72
  web conferencing tools, 164
learning modules, 3, 11, 15, 24, 98, 137
learning theory, 32–33
Link Rot, 15
Listservs, 15, 99, 170
LMS. *See* learning management systems
Lupton-Smith, Helen, 121–123
lurking, 15

marriage and family therapy, websites, 99
massive open online courses, 15
meaningful classroom activities, 116–117
Microsoft PowerPoint, 110
mindfulness, 98–99
Mindmeister, 128, 174
MindTap, 163
mistakes and lessons learned
  crisis management, 134
  engaging passive student, 135
  explicit information, 132–133
  from interruptions, 136
  official email, use of, 135–136
  personal time boundaries, 133
  pets in class, 137
  private chats, 137
  releasing assignments and exams,
    137–138
  right paper to the right student, 136